Teaching Art and Design 3–11

D0524926

Also available from Continuum

Teaching Art and Design 3–11

Edited by **Sue Cox** and **Robert Watts**
with **Judy Grahame**, **Steve Herne**
and **Diarmuid McAuliffe**

Reaching the Standard Series

Series Editor: Mark O'Hara

continuum

Continuum International Publishing Group

The Tower Building   80 Maiden Lane, Suite 704
11 York Road   London   New York,
SE1 7NX   NY 10038

www.continuumbooks.com

British Library Cataloguing-in-Publication Data
A catalogue record for this book is available from the British Library.
ISBN: 0826451101 (paperback)
       0826497179 (hardcover)

Library of Congress Cataloging-in-Publication Data
A catalog record for this book is available from the Library of Congress.

Typeset by Ben Cracknell Studios | www.benstudios.co.uk
Printed and bound in Great Britain by The Cromwell Press, Trowbridge, Wiltshire

Contents

Abbreviations

CGFS Curriculum Guidance for the Foundation Stage
DES Department of Education and Science
DfEE Department for Education and Employment
DfES Department for Education and Skills
ELG Early Learning Goals
ICT Information and Communication Technology
KS1/2 Key Stage 1/2
QCA Qualifications and Curriculum Authority
QTS Qualified Teacher Status
Ofsted Office for Standards in Education
SEN Special educational needs
TDA Training and Development Agency for Schools
TTA Teacher Training Agency

Introduction

This book aims to support student teachers following introductory courses in art and design education, but it will also be useful for those teachers or students who are not receiving or have not received training in the subject. It aims to support the development of teachers' confidence and subject and pedagogical knowledge. It will also provide guidance for beginning teachers and practising teachers who wish to improve their understanding and practice, while subject leaders should find it indispensable as an aid towards developing an overview of art and design, and as a support to developing their leadership and training roles.

The authors of this book are keen to explore the subject of art and design with teachers in a way that acknowledges that we all construct our own understandings through our unique experiences. However, we should be aware that we also pick up on ideas that are shared in society through contact and experience with, for example, family, friends and colleagues in other groups and contexts, as well as through the media. Our understanding is therefore both individually and socially constructed, and we have a great deal of choice about which ideas we adopt and make our own. The authors perceive the subject of art and design as one in a state of flux, partially defined by tradition, but also challenged and redefined by new discoveries and the innovations of artists and designers. What is written about art and design at any given time changes, as does the documentation designed to influence and support teaching and learning in the area. While it is important for students and practising teachers to be familiar with the details of current requirements and guidance, it is equally important to aim to maintain a broader overview of the principles of the subject, together with an open mind that allows us to be creative and to reconstruct and continue to expand our understanding.

Outline of the book

Chapter 1 introduces the subject of art and design and explores concepts of both content and pedagogical knowledge. It presents a rationale for the teaching of the subject and highlights the varied roles art and design can play in people's lives. The views of both children and adults towards the subject are discussed and justifications are identified for the importance and value of the subject in a broad and balanced education.

Chapter 2 covers a range of issues concerned with teaching and learning in art and design. It reflects on the breadth of study of the subject at the Foundation Stage (ages 3–5) and through the primary school (5–11). The English National Curriculum Key Stages are explored with consideration of the importance of transition between them. The chapter explores the historical context of art and design education and the way the subject has developed and surveys the current context that influences how the subject is planned and taught. This is followed by an outline of children's visual development, and consideration of the potential contribution art and design make to the whole curriculum.

Chapter 3 surveys the range of processes in art and design including drawing, painting, printmaking, sculpture, textiles, collage and ICT. This section contains a wealth of detailed guidelines and advice for successful resourcing, planning, management, teaching and learning.

Chapter 4 addresses the issues involved in organizing and managing art and design including timetabling, grouping, links with other subjects, content, record keeping, resourcing and planning of the learning environment.

Chapter 5 examines the planning process. It addresses issues including long-term, medium-term and short-term planning, and emphasizes the importance of sequencing lessons in ways that enable to children to take responsibility for their learning.

Chapter 6 provides a rationale for assessment in art and design; it explores the range of ways in which children's learning can be assessed, and addresses many of the issues that many teachers find challenging about this area.

Chapter 7 addresses the opportunities and challenges posed by engaging with artists' work, and provides strategies for developing children's critical skills in the gallery and the classroom. It is supportive to non-specialists and argues positively for the value and potential for children's learning in this aspect of the art curriculum.

Chapter 8 deals with the issues of equal opportunities in a subject that is often seen as a domain for the gifted and talented rather than a vital part of everyone's life and learning. The chapter explores how we judge children's abilities and discusses the issues of gender, cultural diversity and special educational needs.

At the end of the book you will find an appendix consisting of a list of essential resources for teaching and learning in art and design.

Authors' note

Throughout the book there are references to the National Curriculum, the Curriculum Guidance for the Foundation Stage, the QCA schemes of work for Art and Design and a range of government publications, as well as to a range of published research in the field of art and design education. Specifically, all references are to the English National Curriculum. Unless otherwise specified, readers should assume that the versions of these publications referred to are the latest as of 2006.

Art and Design and the QTS Standards

In order to locate the subject of art and design within the formal requirements of qualifying to teach, we will take a close look at those aspects of the Standards for the Award of Qualified Teacher Status. At the time of writing, the Standards were available in draft form (TTA 2006).

Teaching Standards have a strong bearing on the nature and content of teacher education. They indicate that student teachers must demonstrate a secure knowledge and understanding of the subjects they are trained to teach, and of how to go about teaching them. Despite subject specialisms, every trainee teacher of children aged 3–11 receives training in a broad range of subjects in the curriculum, with many students also trained to teach at the Foundation Stage. All teachers are expected to have 'a sufficient understanding of a range of work' and be able to teach the subject in the age range for which they are trained, 'with advice from an experienced colleague when necessary'.

Meeting the Standards

This book addresses the Standards as follows:

Those recommended for the award of QTS (Q) should:	Induction/main scale teachers (I) should:	Chapter(s)
1. Professional attributes		
Relationships with children and young people		
• Have high expectations of children and young people and a commitment to ensuring that they can achieve their full educational potential and to establishing fair, respectful, trusting, supportive and constructive relationships with them.	• Have high expectations of children and young people including a commitment to ensuring that they can achieve their full educational potential and to establishing fair, respectful, trusting, supportive and constructive relationships with them.	All chapters support high expectations on the part of teachers.
• Demonstrate the positive values, attitudes and behaviour they expect from children and young people.	• Hold positive values and attitudes and adopt high standards of behaviour in their professional role.	All chapters support positive values, attitudes and behaviour on the part of teachers.

Those recommended for the award of QTS (Q) should:	Induction/main scale teachers (I) should:	Chapter(s)
Frameworks		
(a) Be aware of the professional duties of teachers and the statutory framework within which they work.	• Maintain an up-to-date knowledge and understanding of the professional duties of teachers and the statutory framework within which they work, and contribute to the development, implementation and evaluation of the policies and practice of their workplace, including those designed to promote equality of opportunity.	Chapters 1 and 2
(b) Be aware of the policies and practices of the workplace and share in collective responsibility for their implementation.		
Communicating and working with others		
• Communicate effectively with children, young people, colleagues, parents and carers.	(a) Communicate effectively with learners and colleagues.	All chapters support effective communication.
	(b) Communicate effectively with parents and carers, conveying timely and relevant information about attainment, objectives, progress and well-being.	
	(c) Recognize that communication is a two-way process and encourage parents and carers to participate in discussions about the progress, development and well-being of children and young people.	
• Recognize and respect the contribution that colleagues, parents and carers can make to the development and well-being of children and young people and to raising their levels of attainment.	• Recognize and respect the contributions that colleagues, parents and carers can make to the development and well-being of children and young people, and to raising their levels of attainment.	
• Have a commitment to collaboration and cooperative working with colleagues.	• Have a commitment to collaboration and cooperative working where appropriate.	
Personal professional development		
(a) Reflect on and improve their practice, and take responsibility for identifying and meeting their professional development needs.	• Evaluate their performance and be committed to improving their practice through appropriate professional development.	All chapters support reflection and improvement of practice.
(b) Complete a career entry and development profile.		
• Have a creative and constructively critical approach towards innovation; being prepared to adapt their practice where benefits and improvements are identified.	• Have a creative and constructively critical approach towards innovation; being prepared to adapt their practice where benefits and improvements are identified.	All chapters support creative and constructively critical approaches.
• Act upon advice and feedback and be open to coaching and mentoring.	• Act upon advice and feedback and be open to coaching and mentoring.	

Those recommended for the award of QTS (Q) should:	Induction/main scale teachers (I) should:	Chapter(s)

2. Professional knowledge and understanding

Teaching and Learning

• Have a knowledge and understanding of a range of teaching, learning and behaviour management strategies and know how to use and adapt them, including how to personalize learning and provide opportunities for all learners to achieve their potential.	• Have a good, up-to-date working knowledge and understanding of a range of teaching, learning and behaviour management strategies and know how to use and adapt them, including how to personalize the learning experience to provide opportunities for all learners achieve their potential.	Chapters 2 and 8

Assessment and monitoring

(a) Know the assessment requirements and arrangements for the subjects/curriculum areas they are trained to teach, including those relating to public examinations and qualifications.	• Know the assessment requirements and arrangements for the subjects/curriculum areas they teach, including those relating to public examinations and qualifications.	Chapter 6
(b) Be informed of a range of approaches to assessment, including the importance of formative assessment.	• Know a range of approaches to assessment, including the importance of formative assessment.	
(c) Know how to use local and national statistical information to evaluate the effectiveness of their teaching, to monitor the progress of those they teach and to raise levels of attainment.	• Know how to use local and national statistical information to evaluate the effectiveness of their teaching, to monitor the progress of those they teach and to raise levels of attainment.	
	• Know how to use reports and other sources of external information related to assessment in order to provide learners with accurate and constructive feedback on their strengths, weaknesses, attainment, progress and areas for development, including action plans for improvement.	

Subject and curriculum

• Have a secure knowledge and understanding of their subjects/curriculum areas to enable them to teach effectively across the age and ability range for which they are trained to teach.	• Have a secure knowledge and understanding of the subjects/curriculum areas they teach including: the contribution that their subjects/curriculum areas can make to cross-curricular learning, recent relevant developments, and related pedagogy.	Chapters 1, 2, 3 and 7
• Know and understand the relevant statutory and non-statutory curricula, frameworks, including those provided through the National Strategies, for their subjects/curriculum areas, and other relevant initiatives across the age and ability range for which they are trained to teach.	• Know and understand the relevant statutory and non-statutory curricula and frameworks, including those provided through the National Strategies, for their subjects/curriculum areas and other relevant initiatives across the age and ability range they teach.	Chapter 2

Those recommended for the award of QTS (Q) should:	Induction/main scale teachers (I) should:	Chapter(s)
Literacy, numeracy and ICT		
(a) Have passed the professional skills tests in numeracy, literacy and information and communication technology (ICT)	• Know how to use skills in literacy, numeracy and ICT to support their teaching and wider professional activities.	Chapter 3 (ICT)
(b) Know how to use skills in literacy, numeracy and ICT to support their teaching and wider professional activities.		
Achievement and diversity		
• Understand how children develop and that the progress and well-being of learners are affected by a range of developmental, social, religious, ethnic, cultural and linguistic influences.	• Understand how children develop and how the progress, rate of development and well-being of learners are affected by a range of social, religious, ethnic, cultural and linguistic influences.	Chapter 2
• Know how to make effective personalized provision for those they teach in so far as this is practicable, including those for whom English is an additional language, and how to take practical account of diversity and promote equality and inclusion in their teaching.	• Know how to make effective personalized provision for those they teach, including those for whom English is an additional language or who have special educational needs or disabilities, and how to take practical account of diversity and promote equality and inclusion in their teaching.	Chapter 8
• Know and understand the roles of colleagues with specific responsibilities, including those with responsibility for learners with special educational needs and disabilities and other individual learning needs.	• Understand the roles of colleagues such as those having specific responsibilities for learners with special educational needs, disabilities and other individual learning needs, and the contributions they can make to the learning, development and well-being of children and young people.	
	• Know when to draw on the expertise of colleagues, such as those with responsibility for the safeguarding of children and young people and special educational needs and disabilities, and to refer to sources of information, advice and support from external agencies.	
Health and well-being		
(a) Be aware of current legal requirements and policy concerning the well-being of children and young people.	• Know the current legal requirements, national policies and guidance on the safeguarding and promotion of the well-being of children and young people.	
(b) Know how to identify and support children and young people whose progress, development or well-being is affected by changes or difficulties in their personal circumstances, and when to refer them to colleagues for specialist support.	• Know the local arrangements concerning the safeguarding of children and young people.	
	• Know how to identify potential child abuse or neglect and follow safeguarding procedures.	
	• Know how to identify and support children and young people whose progress or well-being is affected by changes or difficulties in their personal circumstances, and when to refer them to colleagues for specialist support.	

Those recommended for the award of QTS (Q) should:	Induction/main scale teachers (I) should:	Chapter(s)
3. Professional skills		

Planning and teaching

(a) Assess the learning needs of those they teach and set challenging learning objectives. (b) Plan and teach lessons and sequences of lessons that are well-organized, demonstrating secure subject knowledge relevant to the curricula across the age and ability range for which they are trained. (c) Use a range of teaching strategies and resources, including e-learning, taking practical account of diversity and promoting equality and inclusion. (d) Provide opportunities for learners to develop their literacy, numeracy and ICT skills.	• Plan and teach challenging, well-organized lessons and sequences of lessons that: • are informed by relevant and up-to-date subject, curriculum and pedagogical knowledge; • use a range of teaching and learning strategies and resources, including e-learning, adapted to meet learners' needs effectively; and • take account of the prior learning and attainment of those they teach and underpin sustained progress and effective transitions. • identify and provide opportunities for learners to develop literacy, numeracy, ICT and thinking and learning skills appropriate within their phase and context.	All chapters support planning and teaching. Chapter 5 deals specifically with planning.
• Provide homework or other out-of-class work to sustain learners' progress and to extend and consolidate their learning.	• Plan, set and assess coursework for examinations, homework and other out-of-class assignments to sustain learners' progress and to extend and consolidate their learning.	

Assessing, monitoring and giving feedback

• Make effective use of a range of assessment, monitoring and recording strategies.	• Make effective use of an appropriate range of observation, assessment, monitoring and recording strategies as a basis for setting challenging learning objectives and monitoring learners' progress and levels of attainment.	Chapter 6
• Provide timely, accurate and constructive feedback on learners' attainment, progress and areas for development.	• Provide learners, colleagues, parents and carers with timely, accurate and constructive feedback on learners' attainment, progress and areas for development. • Support and guide learners so that they can reflect on their learning, identify the progress they have made, set positive targets for improvement and become successful independent learners.	Chapter 6
• Support and guide learners to reflect on their learning, identify the progress they have made and identify their emerging learning needs.	• Use assessment as part of their teaching to diagnose learners' needs, set realistic and challenging targets for improvement and plan future teaching.	Chapter 6

Reviewing teaching and learning

• Evaluate the impact of their teaching on the progress of all learners, and modify their planning and classroom practice where necessary.	• Review the effectiveness of their teaching and its impact on learners' progress, attainment and well-being, refining their approaches where necessary. • Review the impact of the feedback provided to learners and guide learners on how to improve their attainment.	All chapters support reviewing teaching and learning.

Those recommended for the award of QTS (Q) should:	Induction/main scale teachers (I) should:	Chapter(s)
Learning environment		
• Establish a purposeful and safe learning environment conducive to learning and identify opportunities for learners to learn in out of school contexts.	(a) Establish a purposeful and safe learning environment which complies with current legal requirements, national policies and guidance on the safeguarding and well-being of children and young people so that learners feel secure and sufficiently confident to make an active contribution to learning and to the school.	Chapter 4
	(b) Make use of the local arrangements concerning the safeguarding of children and young people.	
	(c) Identify and use opportunities to personalize and extend learning through out of school contexts where possible making links between in-school learning and learning in out-of-school contexts.	
	(a) Manage learners' behaviour constructively by establishing and maintaining a clear and positive framework for discipline, in line with the school's behaviour policy.	
	(b) Use a range of behaviour management techniques and strategies, adapting them as necessary to promote the self-control and independence of learners.	
• Establish a clear framework for classroom discipline to manage learners' behaviour constructively and promote their self-control and independence.	• Promote learners' self-control, independence and cooperation through developing their social, emotional and behavioural skills.	
Team Working and Collaboration		
• Work as a team member and identify opportunities for working with colleagues, sharing the development of effective practice with them.	• Work as a team member and identify opportunities for working with colleagues, managing their work where appropriate and sharing the development of effective practice with them.	Chapter 4
• Ensure that colleagues working with them are appropriately involved in supporting learning and understand the roles they are expected to fulfil.		

Student teachers whose course of study includes the Foundation Stage must also demonstrate that they know and understand the aims and principles of the six areas of learning and the early learning goals described in the Curriculum Guidance for the Foundation Stage (QCA/DfES 2000). The Foundation Stage guidance, aimed at practitioners working with children aged three to five in early years settings such as Nursery and Reception classes, is organized into areas of learning rather than discrete subjects. This acknowledges the overlap and integration of children's learning at this age, which is often developed through informal and constructive play. The area of the guidance with the most relevance to art and design is Creative Development, which, as well as art, also includes aspects of music, dance, role play and imaginative play.

The Standards indicate that student teachers need to know how to use Information and Communication Technology (ICT) within art and design, how to differentiate and accommodate children's special educational needs (SEN) and how to promote good behaviour through appropriate classroom management. Student teachers will need to develop an understanding of issues relating to progression between the Foundation Stage and Key Stages 1 and 2, including, for those training to teach at Key Stage 2, the transition from primary to secondary school. They will also develop an understanding of how child development affects learning; children's visual development is a fascinating area and one of particular importance for those teaching in the early years, as both the understanding of number and of written language has its origins in early mark-making and drawing.

Furthermore, student teachers need to learn how to translate their creative ideas for children's learning into appropriately planned art activities that offer opportunities for assessing and recording children's progress. The planning process requires teachers to take account of the diversity of interests, experiences and achievements of both girls and boys and of pupils from different cultural or ethnic groups, to help all make good progress. It is also important to recognize and to respond to equal opportunities issues, for instance by challenging stereotypical views when exploring cultural traditions or by ensuring access for pupils with disabilities or medical needs. As art and design is a practical subject, health and safety is also an important issue and thought needs to be given to the organization and management of the physical teaching space, tools, materials and other resources so that they are used safely and effectively.

As with any subject taught in schools, teachers are required to be aware of the statutory requirements for teaching and learning as set out in National Curriculum guidelines. In the UK there are, at the time of writing, different arrangements in Scotland, Wales, Northern Ireland and England, although each variation shares a broadly similar conception of the subject. Most developed countries have curriculum documents that can be statutory (they have to be followed and may be the basis for inspection) or advisory/non-statutory (provided as guidelines that leave schools more freedom of choice). This book uses the English National Curriculum (hereinafter referred to as the National Curriculum) documentation for reference, although it will also be highly relevant to other educational contexts throughout the English-speaking world.

Compared with the core subjects of English, mathematics and science, the primary curriculum for art and design is far less prescriptive in nature. This is a positive thing as it is a creative subject and children need space and a measure of freedom to be creative. The National Curriculum Handbook for primary teachers (DfEE/QCA 1999) gives details of the knowledge, skills and understanding that pupils should be taught and breadth of study envisaged. It also sets out the 'knowledge skills and understanding that pupils of different abilities and maturities are expected to have by the end of each key stage' in the form of an Attainment Target statement expressed in a series of level descriptions appropriate to different ages. Further guidance for the curriculum and planning for art and design are contained in the QCA scheme of work for Key Stages 1 and 2 for art and design (DfEE/QCA 2000). These guidelines, though non-statutory, have been widely adopted by schools in the UK.

Bibliography

QCA/DfEE (1999), *The National Curriculum Handbook for Primary Teachers in England – Key Stages 1 and 2*. London: QCA

—— (2000), *Curriculum Guidance for the Foundation Stage.* London: QCA/DfEE.

Useful Websites

www.nc.uk.net/
The National Curriculum online

www.ofsted.gov.uk/publications/annualreport0405/4.1.1.html
The last in a series of reports on primary art and design published by Ofsted.

www.qca.org.uk/223.html
Curriculum Guidance for the Foundation Stage.

www.standards.dfes.gov.uk/schemes2/art/
QCA Schemes of Work for Art and Design at Key Stages 1 and 2.

www.tda.gov.uk
Training and Development Agency for Schools, for full and up to date information on the Standards.

The Subject of Art and Design

This chapter sets out to explore the nature of art and design as a subject that draws upon a variety of contexts and ways of thinking. It examines the attitudes of both adults and children towards the subject, and highlights some of the reasons why art and design is studied in schools. It prompts teachers to reflect upon their knowledge of art and design and of the pedagogical issues surrounding the subject.

What is art and design?

What is the subject of art and design, and what do you know about teaching it? One way to answer this question is to think about your own experience so far in life and to produce a mental map of the subject. Why not try this before reading further? Take a sheet of paper, write 'art and design' in the centre and then suggest as many associated words, concepts, and names as you can to make a spider diagram or flow chart of your ideas and associations. This will represent your current platform of experience of the subject, although you might find out as you read on that you remember more and more!

One way of defining art and design is to say that it is whatever the people on your list do. This definition is open-ended as contemporary artists and designers in the West are often expected to innovate and produce groundbreaking and challenging work that questions and expands existing categories and understandings. Artists respond to contexts of past art and culture which are documented in a range of disciplines such as art history, cultural studies and archaeology. Art historians present influential stories of how art has developed, how artists have advanced modern art by building on each other's discoveries. Critics, however, have questioned these stories as being the product of powerful Western dominating cultural influences that have in turn disenfranchised others. If you return to your list of artists, how many are 'dead white European men'? Are there fewer women artists, or artists from non-Western cultures and traditions? Does fine art feature far more than design or craft, and painting more than ceramics or textiles? The more you share your thoughts and experiences with others, the more opportunities you will have to question the hierarchies that have been established.

The process of gathering your ideas about art and design should have prompted you to consider the range of processes that children engage with in school. Drawing and painting will spring quickly to most people's minds. A longer list would include printmaking, collage, sculpture, perhaps textiles and even photography or digital media. In a way we are defining the subject by the names given to the practices associated with it, characterized by the materials and processes used. The National Curriculum for Art and Design (DfEE 1999) requires that pupils should be taught using a range of materials and processes, in projects involving two and three dimensions and on different scales. It does not have a statutory list of practices, but gives the following examples: painting, collage, printmaking, digital media, textiles and sculpture.

Developing subject content knowledge for teaching children aged 3–11 will ideally involve developing a familiarity with all of these practices, and Chapter 3 explores each of them in turn. Many of us also think instinctively of the people who make art and design: the artists, designers, craftspeople, sculptors, architects, photographers, etc. If you have not already included these, give yourself two minutes to make a separate list on a sheet of paper of the names of as many of these creative people from the past and present as you can think of.

The National Curriculum indicates that the subject art and design includes 'art, design and craft'. It recommends no particular artists or cultural traditions that must be taught, but the programmes of study state that 'pupils should be taught about the differences and similarities in the work of the artists, craftspeople and designers . . . their roles and purposes . . . . in different times and cultures' (DfEE 1999, p. 120). This means that teachers are quite free to choose the artists and cultures that they introduce to their pupils, although they need to do this by drawing on the principle of a broad and balanced curriculum and the 'global perspective' implied by this.

Art and design also takes its place in the family of subjects called the Arts, which are usually thought of as including visual arts, dance, drama, music, literature and digital and lens-based media. This may include some input from art and design, for example, in relation to drama, in the form of costume, set and prop design, theatrical lighting and graphic design for tickets, brochures and posters. Thinking about the similarities and differences between the different arts forms is a valuable way of refining our understanding of the subject and, clearly, when we begin to look at cross-curricular connections between subjects, those between the arts are powerful. The term visual arts (or visual and tactile arts) is often used as a broad umbrella term for the subject. However, some theorists are now beginning to write about 'visual culture education' as a term for the future of an expanded subject that could include the experience that young people need in order to be critical consumers and producers in our contemporary age.

Through gathering your ideas about art and design you may have identified words such as line, tone, colour, etc. These are often called the 'visual and tactile elements' or just the 'elements of art'. The list provided in the National Curriculum for art and design is: *colour, pattern, texture, line, tone, shape, form and space.*

Some forms of art and design contain just one or two of these elements: for instance, a line drawing that defines shape. Other forms may use several, for instance, a painting made using of colour, pattern and texture to define form and space. Some people think of art and design as a visual *language,* and in this context the visual elements are the building blocks or visual and tactile 'vocabulary': the 'letters and words' which in combination allow all sorts of expressive and communicative possibilities. Understanding what these terms mean through experimentation and investigation, recognizing them in works of art and being able to use them as a visual language to express feelings and ideas, and create images and artefacts, has been a long-term aim of art education in Britain since the 1950s. More recently, some art educators have criticized this approach, when it leads to formal exercises divorced from personal artistic impulses and the creation of meaningful work.

Where can we find art and design?

An obvious response to this question would be 'in museums and galleries'. Yet is it a valuable exercise to explore further the nature of art and design by thinking about the wider range of places and institutions where it can be found around us. Almost everything that is manufactured is designed, the clothes that we are wearing, the furniture, equipment and textiles of our interior spaces. The streets are our most accessible 'art gallery', where the visual styles of the past and present are expressed through the changing technology of building materials, methods and design. Gothic churches are juxtaposed with Victorian terraces, while the 1920s' Art-Deco shopfront competes with contemporary modernism in our high streets. Architectural crafts, tiles and stone-carving animate facades, and decorative ironwork provides barriers. The great and the good are commemorated in bronze statues and war memorials, while contemporary sculptures adorn public spaces.

Art galleries and museums provide spaces for study and contemplation, preserve cultural memory or provoke debate about the nature of art, beauty, identity, culture and society.

Poster shops in the high street sell reproductions of artists' work and iconic images that allow us to define our identities by providing choice in what to display in our living spaces. Newsagents display hundreds of magazines focusing on increasingly differentiated interests and lifestyles, creating a glossy visual culture of type and photography. Art colleges offer hundreds of art and design courses in fine art, graphic design, product design, textiles, fashion, etc., providing a hotbed of creativity and new ideas and new recruits who feed into the ever-increasing arts and media industries which shape our contemporary culture.

Adults' views of art and design

Increasing attendances at museums and galleries such as Tate Modern suggest that many adults hold positive views about art and design and perhaps understand that some of the highest achievements of humanity are preserved in the material culture of past and present civilizations. Levels of public awareness of contemporary art are high, thanks in part to the increasingly high profile of displays such as the Saatchi Collection and the annual Turner Prize exhibition at Tate Britain. However, many people remain sceptical about the seriousness of some contemporary artists and, encouraged by sections of the media and suspecting a confidence trick, ridicule works such as Damien Hirst's pickled shark and Tracey Emin's unmade bed.

Nationally, the creative industries have overtaken manufacturing in economic importance; imagination and creativity are highly desirable qualities in the jobseeker's market. The subject of art and design, however, remains low on the priority list in schools amidst assumptions which promote 'basic skills', such as literacy and numeracy and the acquisition of factual knowledge above the arts, leaving art as a Friday afternoon treat or a reward when the 'proper' work is complete (Herne 2000). Thus, visual and tactile modes of meaning making and communication, the aesthetic curriculum and the education of feelings (the 'affective' curriculum) are undervalued. There is no guarantee that children are being provided with the broad and balanced curriculum to which they are entitled. Students, class teachers and subject leaders may have to confront a range of negative assumptions and articulate persuasive arguments in order to give their pupils access to a relevant and valuable art and design education.

Despite clear evidence of the relatively low status of the subject within the primary curriculum (Herne, 2000), there is evidence that many teachers have a thoughtful and reflective approach towards teaching and learning in the subject. Downing *et al.* (2003) surveyed the attitudes and experiences of head teachers and class teachers in the UK towards teaching the arts in primary schools and concluded that: 'The most highly endorsed purposes . . . were to develop creative and thinking skills and . . . communication and expressive skills. These were followed by purposes associated specifically with learning in the arts, which were ahead of purposes associated with personal development . . . many head teachers viewed the arts as central to raising standards in schools' (p. 1). Downing *et al.*'s report presented a picture in which the aims of well-meaning teachers were frustrated by the constraints of an unsympathetic system: the implication being that, given sufficient time and resources, a clear improvement in the provision for art and design in primary schools would take place: 'While not revealed in any performance tables or end of key stage tests, head teachers and class teachers were convinced of the value of the arts in education and seemed determined to ensure their continued contribution to the education of the whole child and the welfare of schools' (ibid. p. 3). It is clear that, despite the scepticism to be found in some areas of society, art is a subject that teachers recognize as occupying an important place in the primary curriculum and at the Foundation Stage.

Children's approaches towards art and design

Very young children are naturally experimental and soon begin to learn to control their responses to a wide range of stimuli. Experimentation with all kinds of objects and materials in the world, as well as sound, movement and mark making, are a natural creative part of learning for very young children. Well-resourced Foundation Stage settings provide bricks, sand, water, toys, construction kits and materials, books and computers as well as the range of media associated with art and design such as clay, paint, crayons, printing media, 'cutting and sticking' materials, etc. These art resources provide young children with a way of gaining experience about how the world looks and feels, a means of developing thinking and powers of communication and media for expressing ideas and feelings. Children explore the materials and their properties, cause and effect and how things work and can combine. They develop many concepts through these early playful encounters and experiences, through investigating, experimenting, looking, making, discussing and thinking. At the Foundation Stage, children are introduced to school subjects with particular practices, routines and language. By the time children reach the end of the primary phase they can develop quite complex understandings of art and design, its scope and uses, drawing on information from school, their family, through mass communication media and the internet.

Researching 10- and 11-year-olds' attitudes towards art and design in Cyprus, Pavlou (2006) found that art was a satisfying and fulfilling subject for the pupils in the study. Many drew at home and defined art as a motivating, worthwhile and productive activity. They perceived it as a subject that required demanding thinking as well as practical activity. Some pupils believed that the thinking that was required to express or represent their ideas was different to the kind required in other subjects such as maths or languages. They saw it as a pleasurable, important and serious activity. Art was most enjoyable when they could relax and feel a sense of control over their work. Art and design was important because it offered them knowledge, skills and a chance to express themselves. It appeared that the subject was experienced as an intrinsically rewarding activity: they devoted time and effort to it because they appreciated the quality of experience they gained from the 'flow' of total involvement in the act of thinking and making.

Recent research in the UK (Watts 2005) reveals that most children claim that the main reason why they make art is simply because they enjoy it, while they believe that the main reason why adults make art is to make money. However, when these children were asked why they thought art was *important*, neither of these reasons featured strongly in their responses: instead, they talked about themes of communication, aesthetics and personal development. The implication here is that as teachers we should not underestimate children's potential for taking on board a range of serious and quite complex ideas about art and education.

Why study art and design?

Art and design occupies a unique place at the Foundation Stage and in the primary curriculum for a range of reasons:

1 It offers children opportunities to develop a range of skills, techniques and practices, some of which date back centuries while others are contemporary in nature.

2 It is a unique visual and tactile language with a set of elements that can be combined to make possible powerful visual statements.

3 Through developing as artists, designers and critics, children can develop skills which make them 'visually literate', learning about ways of interpreting and responding to works of art.

4 Art and design offers potential for individual expression that satisfies a human need to communicate; this can provide deep satisfaction and promote mental balance and well-being.

5 A core of observation work can provide a study skill, training in precise looking, concentration and visual and tactile sensitivity.

6 Art and design develops an understanding of the creative process which is highly valued, not only in itself, but also as a transferable skill in contemporary life and work

7 Being introduced to art and culture with a global perspective develops cultural awareness, sensitivity and appreciation of diversity; this is sometimes called 'cultural literacy'.

8 Practical art activity and critical response to artists' work develop intellectual and aesthetic awareness and design skills which are worthwhile in themselves as well as useful in everyday life and employment.

Art and design: pedagogical knowledge

Pedagogical knowledge focuses on how to teach the subject and how to facilitate children's learning and experience in the classroom. It is the kind of knowledge and understanding which takes you beyond your own practice of art activities. It requires you to learn how to introduce ideas or activities to children, how to effectively demonstrate techniques, how to resource learning through an effective choice of media and the optimal ways of organizing and managing a classroom for practical work. You also need to know how to introduce children to artists work through careful questioning, sustained looking and discussion. This kind of subject knowledge is therefore really about the *craft* of the classroom.

Developing pedagogical subject knowledge requires that you first develop an ability to undertake a particular art activity yourself. This will enable you to identify the steps needed in a particular process, the equipment, the materials, concepts and experience that support this particular creative activity. When preparing for teaching, even if you are familiar with the particular activity, it is a very good idea to try out yourself what you are going to do with the children with the equipment and tools that are available to you in a school. This process will enable you to make sure that you haven't forgotten any vital items of equipment that you might need, it will give you practice if you are going to demonstrate anything and it will also develop your confidence and fresh, recent experience. You will be able to discuss your own experiences with the children during your introduction and during the lesson, when you are interacting with the children on a more individual level.

Practical workshops that you engage with on initial teacher education courses or, if you are a serving teacher, continuing professional development courses, should also model effective ways of organizing and teaching art activities. Another important way of exploring how these activities are best taught in class is by observing an experienced practitioner in school. Not all class teachers are confident art and design teachers but it is usually possible to find one or two members of staff who are confident and effective and would welcome your participant observation!

It is important to consider how particular practices, for instance, painting, are explored at different ages and stages. At the Foundation Stage children have playful experiential encounters with paint. Painting easels are set up vertically with paints available, and at other times children can paint working horizontally on a table. They may also be able to do hand and finger painting, or work on a larger scale outdoors. Usually they are free to choose what to paint and explore all sorts of personal concerns with the nature of liquid, mark making and designing with lines and shapes. At other times they can be challenged to make a response to something they are looking at, for instance the patterns in leaves, during a teacher-supported focus activity. Even young children can learn how to use a set of paints quite carefully and to mix their own colours, and should not be denied this opportunity. As children move on to Key Stage 1 they can learn how to match colours from direct observation or learn more about how to use their painting skills in an expressive way. As children progress to Key Stage 2 they can refine their painting skills, explore different approaches and combine ideas to create more complex pieces of work. An understanding of characteristic ways of working and expectations at different ages and stages is vitally important in planning for children's progression and effectively differentiating the work set for them. It allows teachers to plan for the appropriate amount of input and challenge, to accommodate children who need support or those who are gifted and talented. Observation in schools is a key to developing this understanding and comparison between schools is also very valuable in identifying well-informed expectations.

Summary

Your subject-content knowledge and pedagogical knowledge is effectively consolidated when you have a chance to teach a particular activity in school. As a student you will often be offered opportunities to teach small groups of children before moving on to whole-class teaching. This can be a very good way of gaining experience and building confidence. You will quickly become aware that things don't always go according to plan, or are not completely successful. This is a valuable chance to reflect on what went well, what did not go so well, to think about why and make constructive plans for the future. Skills of evaluation and reflection are crucial for both the student and practising teacher: a 'reflective practitioner' can continually refine their classroom skills throughout their career. While practical lessons – whether they are art and design, design and technology or science – may present teachers with particular management and organizational challenges, they are essential to the curriculum because they involve direct experience and offer great opportunities to enhance children's enjoyment, increase their motivation and develop their learning.

Box 1.1 Audit your own Subject Knowledge

Record your own level of experience in relation to subject-content knowledge and pedagogical knowledge, profile your existing repertoire; this will help you to target areas in which you need further experience and development.

Previous art education/training

- Can you remember and describe some of your art activities/learning in primary school? At secondary school?
- Describe a memorable feature of any art education you received at secondary level and post-16.

Art activities

- Have you done or do you do any self–directed art activities?

Creative activities

- Are you involved in any creative activities that include an aesthetic dimension (cooking, gardening, home decorating, making clothes, etc.)?

Relevant experience

- Any other experience you feel is relevant?

Books

- Have you read any books or articles on art education theory or practice? If so, please list.

Favourites

- Who or what are your favourite artists, designers, craftspeople, movements, styles, cultural traditions?

Interests

- What other areas of the arts or popular culture are you interested in?

Bibliography

DfEE (1999), *The National Curriculum: Handbook for Primary Teachers in England Key Stages 1 and 2*. London: QCA

—— (2000). *Curriculum Guidance for the Foundation Stage*, DfEE/QCA.

Downing, D., Johnson, F. and Kaur, S. (2003), *Saving a Place for the Arts? A Survey of the Arts in Primary Schools in England (Research Summary)*. Slough: National Foundation for Educational Research.

Harland, J. K., Lord, K., and P. Stott, A. (2000), *Arts Education in Secondary Schools: Effects and Effectiveness*. Slough: NFER.

Herne, S. (2000), 'Breadth and balance? The impact of the National Literacy and Numeracy Strategies on art in the primary school', *The International Journal of Art & Design Education* 19(2): 217–23.

Pavlou, V. (2006), 'Pre-adolescents' perceptions of competence, motivation and engagement in art activities' *The International Journal of Art and Design Education*, 25(2): 194–204.

Read, H. (1943), *Education Through Art*. London: Faber and Faber.

Teacher Training Agency (2002), *Professional Standards for Qualified Teacher Status and Requirements for Initial Teacher Training*. London: TTA.

Watts, R. (2005), 'Attitudes to making art in the primary school', *The International Journal of Art and Design Education*, 24(3), 243–53.

Art and Design in Foundation and Primary Settings

2

Chapter Outline

This chapter discusses the nature of creativity and the value of art and design, as well as placing the curriculum in its historical context to provide insight into its current form. It looks at the breadth of study in art and design, from the Foundation Stage through to Key Stage 2. It introduces the *Curriculum Guidance for the Foundation Stage* (QCA/DfEE 2000) and the statutory requirements of the English National Curriculum for Art and Design (DfEE/QCA 1999) and discusses children's development across the Foundation Stage and Key Stages 1 and 2.

Creativity in art and design

One definition of creativity is that used by the National Advisory Committee on Creative and Cultural Education in its report *All Our Futures* (NACCCE 1999). In this seminal report, commissioned by the government to inquire into the state of creative and cultural education in the UK and to make recommendations for the development of principles, policies and practice for our education system, creativity was defined as 'Imaginative activity fashioned so as to produce outcomes that are both original and of value' (p. 29). Whether we are looking at art and design at the Foundation Stage or at Key Stage 1 or 2 it is best to think of creativity in terms of a series of processes. The creative processes selected in the *All Our Futures* report have four characteristics:

> First, they always involve thinking or behaving *imaginatively*. Second, overall this imaginative activity is *purposeful*: that is, it is directed to *achieve* an objective. Third, these processes must generate something *original*. Fourth, the outcome must be of *value* in relation to the objective.
>
> (ibid., p. 29)

Unlike previous curriculum reforms, this report provides a theoretical framework for creativity in education that underpins the recommendations made. It is important to recognize that creativity is not exclusive to art and design, but is characteristic of all areas of knowledge. There is a tendency to talk of creativity only in relation to the arts, but of course it has wider application. Children can learn to be creative in science and mathematics in ways appropriate to those subjects. As it is manifested in distinctive ways in different areas, in the context of art and design creativity must be thought of in terms of the subject's particular ways of thinking and knowing.

Among art educators there is currently a strong awareness and appreciation of art and design as process. Many attempts have been made to pin down and articulate the creative process through which intuition, imagination and creativity are released. The best way to understand the creative process in art and design and become confident in its practice is to engage in it over and over again in different contexts. The creative process can be seen in its more rational form in the design process, where it is used to investigate human needs and design useful artefacts, or it can be seen in its more personal, expressive form when artists use it to communicate ideas and feelings, to critically explore issues to or provoke debate.

The value of art and design within the curriculum and across Key Stages

Teachers need to provide sufficient time and space for their pupils to explore being creative in art and design, and to provide and preserve a learning environment that embraces risk taking – which is a core value within art and design. Art and design processes are featured in two areas of the *Curriculum Guidance for the Foundation Stage* (DfEE/QCA 2000). Drawing, for example, exists as an element in the area of Communication, Language and Literacy, though, curiously, is not explicitly mentioned in the area of Creative Development. The guidance for the area of the former suggests early years practitioners 'encourage children to draw and paint and talk to them about what they have done' (ibid., p. 65); it also states that children should learn how to 'draw lines and circles using gross motor movement' (ibid., p. 66). In the area of Creative Development it is suggested that children should 'differentiate marks and movement on paper' (ibid., p. 120), while one Early Learning Goal states that they should 'express and communicate their ideas, thoughts and feelings by using a widening range of materials, suitable tools (etc.) . . .' (ibid., p. 126). It is worth noting that the inclusion of drawing under Communication, Language and Literacy serves to suggest that drawing is seen and valued as a prewriting skill and possibly is not considered as vital a form of communication as the child's use of words. Anning and Ring (2004), in their recent study of young children's drawing behaviour state that

> children should not be made to feel that drawing is only a 'temporary' holding form of symbolic representation leading to mastery of the 'higher level' ability to form letters and numbers. The importance of drawing in its own right should be acknowledged and conveyed to children.
>
> (ibid., p. 118).

We know from our observations of young children that they naturally engage in meaning making in a multitude of ways, employing all their senses in pursuit of a greater understanding of the world around them. Since 1998, however, schools in the UK have been under increased pressure to raise standards in literacy and numeracy, arguably to the detriment of other subjects such as art and design. There is some evidence that, with the introduction of the National Literacy and Numeracy Strategies, children entering formal education, especially those moving into Key Stage 1, had less time to explore and enjoy learning in the foundation subjects, including art and design (Herne 2000). Time, attention, training and resources were diverted towards the core subjects and away from the foundation subjects, including art and design. Teachers should aim to ensure that, despite this emphasis on raising standards in literacy and numeracy, children are given opportunities to access a balanced and open cultural and visual education and that teachers find the time within the school day to achieve this. With the implementation of the Primary Strategy (DfES 2003) there are increasing levels of interest in creativity and a refocusing on 'excellence and enjoyment' in the primary curriculum which some see as a chance to open up more space again for the subject.

Primary teachers with responsibility for the whole curriculum need to work and think across all subject areas. Art and design lend themselves to working across and through subject disciplines. Through developing children's competence in the use of art and design media, teachers can extend children's ability to communicate in 'multimodal' ways (Kress 1997). Kress has made a significant contribution to the development of literacy and the relationship between different forms of representation and writing. His work, and that of Matthews (1999; 2003), has much to say to teachers about the value of drawing, for instance, and has implications for how drawing activity might be perceived across the curriculum. Kress's writings have prompted discussions on the role of drawing within the teaching of literacy in schools and thus have helped to bring art and design into theoretical discussions of learning in general.

Kress (1997) makes clear that the world cannot be known only through written language (p. xix) but that we must recognize that children act multimodally: that in some instances the best way of representing meaning is through language, but in others a more appropriate approach might be through the use of other media, such as drawing, painting, model making or construction. In any case, we must be mindful that 'many modes of representation are always in use at the same time' (ibid., p. 38), and that teachers need to recognize and be sensitive towards children's attempts at making meaning. That is, teachers need to show children that they appreciate their creations by taking an interest in them and inquiring into how they were made, the ideas behind them and the materials used in their creation. By providing a sensitive and well-balanced approach to the art and design curriculum, teachers can enable children to find a means of personal expression and identity through engaging with art and design materials and processes.

As argued elsewhere in this book, art and design provides an alternative way of thinking and learning about the world around us. Creativity through art and design helps children to keep an open mind, to take risks and to recognize that there is no one right answer or solution to the challenges that they face in art and design. Questioning and challenging assumptions are an integral part of creativity, critical thinking and art and design and these qualities are transferable into all subject areas. Children can use knowledge gained in art and design to explore and develop at a deeper level the full range of subjects studied at school. Evidence suggests that a growing number of schools are now using arts techniques, experiences, activities and teaching strategies to raise standards in other lessons (QCA 2005). When working across two or more subject areas children can develop skills and qualities that improve their attainment across the curriculum and children's attitudes to learning improve when their self-confidence is increased and they are given a sense of achievement.

A report on the effect and effectiveness of arts education (Harland 2000), although focusing on the secondary phase for its research data, sums up nicely the broad positive outcomes of arts, and therefore art education. The report found that there were a number of 'intrinsic and immediate effects' including a sense of enjoyment, excitement, fulfilment, stress reduction and therapeutic value. There were developments of 'art-form knowledge and skills' in terms of enhanced knowledge, understanding, appreciation and skills. Learners developed 'knowledge in the social and cultural domains' relating to the broadening of pupil perspectives on cultural traditions and diversity, environmental contexts and surroundings and social and moral issues. They developed 'creativity and thinking skills and problem-solving strategies'. Learners developed 'communication and expressive skills' including outcomes associated with the enrichment of interactive communication skills, language competency, interpretative and active listening skills and the capacity to use expressive skills to make statements about themselves and their worlds. Their 'personal and social development' was positively affected, their intra- and interpersonal awareness and skills were heightened, including the sense of self and identity, self-esteem, self-confidence and teamwork skills. They were more aware of others and their needs, and more able to develop rounded and balanced personalities.

The curriculum for art and design: the historical context

In the past, art and design education policy in the West has swung between a utilitarian and a liberal approach. A utilitarian approach stresses the importance of art (and particularly design) education's role in serving society through providing superior manufactured goods that can triumph in the global economy. This orientation was particularly evident in the 'National Course for Instruction' which was developed by Henry Cole in 1836 for the first state-sponsored art college in England which was to become The Royal College of Art (Macdonald 2004). At the same time Cole developed a collection of designed objects and artefacts, a kind of repository of examples of 'good design' that was later to become the Victoria and Albert Museum. An echo of this period was felt in the 'design boom' of the 1980s under Margaret Thatcher's promotion of the market economy and 'Great Britain plc'. Design was again seen as a way of increasing competitiveness and economic success.

The liberal approach stresses the humanizing and civilizing effects of practising 'arts for art's sake': the self-realization that comes through creative and aesthetic work is valued as an end in itself. The human development that is promoted through art activity is part of the work of realising each person's full potential. This approach was evident in the widespread use of art activities in the child-centred approaches to education in the 1960s, and the continuing emphasis on the communicative and expressive potential of art.

The reader might consider which of these public traditions or two broad approaches has been more influential in their own art education. As adults, it can be useful to interrogate our own experience, conceptions and views about art and design, as they can become useful sources of subject knowledge for our own teaching. Conversely, if we have acquired negative or biased views about art and design we may need to restructure our approach and question these conceptions, lest we inadvertently pass on our prejudices or misconceptions to children.

In the second half of the nineteenth century, drawing on Henry Cole's National Course for Instruction, special illustrated cards were produced for primary schools, so that children, like adults, could develop their drawing skills through copying. The 'child art movement' of the 1930s and 40s reacted against this and brought in a child-centred approach, which influenced Herbert Read to write *Education Through Art* (1993), a key text in which he set out his ideas for what he believed to be an appropriate art education for children that represented the new thinking. He believed that children should have the opportunity to express themselves through making images and objects which communicated personal ideas and feelings. He also believed that children should be given the opportunity to undertake objective studies, to draw and paint from observation, which he regarded as essential training for both the eye and the brain. Thirdly, he believed that children should learn to appreciate the work made by a range of artists and designers.

Art educators and theorists have tried to define the scope of art and design by identifying its essential component aspects, arguing that the curriculum models produced could be used as the bases for the rational planning of the subject. Read's curriculum model (1943) can be expressed simply as follows:

Self-expression   Observation   Appreciation
                                                                                (Read 1943)

Each of these areas is still regarded as important in today's National Curriculum. However, Read saw these three strands as existing almost like separate unconnected courses, whereas today, appreciation – exploring the work of artists, designers or craftspeople – is interrelated with the work the children are going to design and make themselves and integrated into a creative sequence of activities.

The 1960s saw the growth of a movement known as 'visual education', promoted by a government-appointed curriculum development group called the Schools Council. Reacting to what some saw as the unstructured learning approach of the 'child art movement', educators argued for a more structured use of observational drawing as the starting point for learning across the curriculum. Educators saw how children, when engaged in direct observation, noticed much more about the things they studied and began to ask more questions. Observational drawing, it was argued, could become central to the curriculum and the questions that arose through drawing could become starting points for children's further study in history, science, mathematics, etc. This approach suited the child-centred philosophy and the integrated topic or project approach that emerged in the planning for young children's work during this period. The teacher aimed to facilitate this process by providing a range of interesting and varied visual resources such as natural forms, so that children could study the structure and patterns of nature. Household equipment, old machines which could be taken apart, tools, historical and cultural artefacts, etc. were all regarded as potentially valuable starting points for children's self-motivated learning. The rallying cry of this movement was 'working from direct experience'; children learnt from first-hand experience rather than relying on the second-hand experience of copying from books or on 'self-expression' alone as a means of developing their abilities. Teachers who employed these methods noticed that children's observation skills improved and that they were able to concentrate on looking for longer periods of time. Their representational drawing skills consequently improved and they were challenged to find more inventive marks and qualities in the art media to respond to the nuances of what was being drawn and observed.

During the 1980s a change began to take place in secondary art education that led to a greater integration of the appreciation of art and cultural traditions into the creative process of student's own art making. Students not only learnt some art history but also began to learn about ways of discussing art. The works they studied were often thematically linked to their own practical projects in order that they could learn about a particular artist's work or a cultural tradition and apply this knowledge to their own creative art work. This kind of knowledge and understanding of artists' work became an important part of the National Curriculum which was introduced in 1992, and was adapted for the primary art and design curriculum. It was a new emphasis in primary art education and continues to be an important aspect of the subject (see Chapter 7).

The curriculum for art and design: the current context

The earlier version of *Art in the National Curriculum (England)* was first introduced in 1992 (DES/HMSO 1992). Its introduction prompted many local education authorities to provide subject training for teachers in primary schools and during this period research has shown (Herne 2000) that a new seriousness and professionalism was brought to the subject. The quality of the practice of the subject subsequently improved in most schools and some particularly interesting cross-curricular work emerged, as well as work in which art was treated as a discrete subject in its own right. In many ways the current QCA scheme of work for art and design (DfEE/QCA 2000) represents the fruits of the curriculum development that went on during this period.

There is arguably a much wider diversity of practice of art and design in the primary phase now than there was during the earlier phase of the introduction of the National Curriculum (Ofsted 2004). Generally, however, good practice is patchy and this provides particular challenges to student teachers and teachers who may not feel as well supported in developing their expertise in art and design as they do in the core subjects. Subject leaders need to develop strong skills of advocacy to create fertile ground for their subject to develop. For example, many schools that are concerned about under-achievement against nationally set targets, are encouraged to focus strongly on teaching the core subjects, leaving pupils with few opportunities for creative and practical experience in their educational diet. However, others have embraced the arts as a way of preserving the education of the 'whole child', motivating and enriching lives, as an alternative route to high standards and achievement. Initiatives such as the Artsmark Awards (Arts Council 2006a) provided a process through which many schools gained recognition for their arts curriculum, while 'Creative Partnerships' (Arts Council 2006b) were set up to develop creativity across the curriculum through partnerships between schools and professional artists and arts organizations.

Teachers are now strongly encouraged to make cross-curricular links between art and design and other subject areas. There is potential for making connections with the English curriculum, for instance, developing children's understanding of non-fiction texts through researching the work of other artists and focusing on skills in speaking and listening when talking about their own work and that of others. Similarly, there are clear links between art and design and mathematics around the concepts of shape and space.

The curriculum for the Foundation Stage

Curriculum Guidance for the Foundation Stage (QCA/DfEE 2000) clearly acknowledges creativity as fundamental to successful learning. This is exemplified through its inclusion as one of the six area of learning, Creative Development, which encompasses art, music, dance, role play and imaginative play.

Box 2.1 To give all children the best opportunity for effective creative development, practitioners should give particular attention to:

1 a stimulating environment in which creativity, originality and expressiveness are valued;
2 a wide range of activities that children can respond to by using many senses;
3 sufficient time for children to explore, develop ideas and finish working at their ideas;
4 opportunities for children to express their ideas through a wide range of types of representation;
5 resources from a variety of cultures to stimulate different ways of thinking;
6 opportunities to work alongside artists and other creative adults;
7 opportunities for children with visual impairment to access and have physical contact with artefacts, material, spaces and movements;
8 opportunities for children with hearing impairment to experience sound through physical contact with instruments and other sources of sound;
9 opportunities for children who cannot communicate by voice to respond to music in different ways, such as gestures;
10 accommodating children's specific religious or cultural beliefs relating to particular forms of art or methods of representation.

(QCA/DFEE 2000, p. 116)

The Foundation Stage guidance highlights the two areas of learning and teaching.

Effective learning, it suggests, involves 'children having time to explore and experiment with ideas, materials and activities'; 'children feeling secure to try new experiences and ways of doing things' and 'children learning through all of their senses' (ibid., p. 117). Effective teaching, we would argue, involves facilitating these experiences and providing a safe and secure environment in which to learn, as well as providing appropriate teacher support through interaction. The guidance stresses the need for time, that is, time to make mistakes and to try out innovative ideas – in other words, time to be creative. It cautions against any attempt at short-circuiting the creative process for the purpose of 'instant results'. It is best to always bear in mind that *process* is far more important to the child's learning and development than final *product* – it is in the process of making and thinking that children develop and learn most effectively in art and design. Too much emphasis has often been placed on end product, with the result that many teachers avoid altogether the often messy nature of the process and opt instead for what they see to be a less risky art activity that will deliver the clean and slick end product.

Box 2.2 Effective teaching requires:

1 practitioners who give children opportunities to develop their own ideas;
2 valuing children's own ideas and not expecting them to reproduce someone else's picture, dance, model or recipe;
3 practitioners who plan experiences, opportunities and the environment to support children's ability to discover, explore and express their creativity;
4 practitioners who interact with and support children in developing confidence, independence in making choices and children's response to what they see, hear, smell touch and feel.

(QCA/DfEE 2000, p. 118)

Curriculum Guidance for the Foundation Stage sets out Early Learning Goals for all of the six areas of learning: Personal, Social and Emotional Development; Communication. Language and Literacy; Mathematical Development; Knowledge and Understanding of the World; Physical Development; Creative Development. It is stressed that these 'establish the expectations for most children to reach by the end of the Foundation Stage, but [they] are not a curriculum in themselves' (ibid. 2000, p. 26).

> **Box 2.3 In the area of creative development the Early Learning Goals that relate to art and design in particular are for children to:**
>
> 1 explore colour, texture, shape, form and space in two or three dimensions
> 2 use their imagination in art and design
> 3 respond in a variety of ways to what they see, hear, smell, touch and feel
> 4 express and communicate their ideas, thoughts and feeling using a widening range of materials, suitable tools, imaginative and role play, movement, designing and making (ibid. p.120–6).
>
> In the Guidance document each of these is supported by more detailed descriptions of 'stepping stones' that mark progress towards these goals.

What children can do with some very basic materials should not be underestimated. For example, we see how in the early years children begin to work up drawings from simple hand and fingerprints, and begin to engage in freehand drawing to create all manner of imagery. Whether it is simply drawing with a pencil or inking up their index finger, young children should be encouraged to see that their own creative play can be represented and made meaningful through art and design.

Art and Design at Key Stages 1 and 2: The National Curriculum

> **Box 2.4 Key Stages 1 and 2**
>
> *Key Stage 1*
>
> **Knowledge, skills and understanding**
>
> Teaching should ensure that 'investigating and making' includes 'exploring and developing ideas' and 'evaluating and developing work'. 'Knowledge and understanding' should inform this process.
>
> **Exploring and developing ideas**
>
> Pupils should be taught to:
> a. record from first-hand observation, experience and imagination, and explore ideas
> b. ask and answer questions about the starting points for their work, and develop their ideas.

Investigating and making art, craft and design

Pupils should be taught to:
a. investigate the possibilities of a range of materials and processes
b. try out tools and techniques, and apply these to materials and processes, including drawing
c. represent observations, ideas and feelings, and design and make images and artefacts.

Evaluating and developing work

Pupils should be taught to:
a. review what they and others have done and say what they think and feel about it
b. identify what they might change in their current work or develop in their future work.

Knowledge and understanding

Pupils should be taught about:
a. visual and tactile elements, including colour, pattern and texture, line and tone, shape, form and space
b. materials and processes used in making art, craft and design
c. differences and similarities in the work of artists, craftspeople and designers in different times and cultures (for example, sculptors, photographers, architects, textile designers).

Breadth of study

During the Key Stage, pupils should be taught the Knowledge, skills and understanding through:
a. exploring a range of starting points for practical work (for example, themselves, their experiences, stories, natural and made objects and the local environment)
b. working on their own, and collaborating with others, on projects in two and three dimensions and on different scales
c. using a range of materials and processes (for example, painting, collage, printmaking, digital media, textiles, sculpture)
d. investigating different kinds of art, craft and design (for example, in the locality, in original and reproduction form, during visits to museums, galleries and sites, on the internet).

Notes

During Key Stage 1 pupils develop their creativity and imagination by exploring the visual, tactile and sensory qualities of materials and processes. They learn about the role of art, craft and design in their environment. They begin to understand colour, shape and space and pattern and texture, and use them to represent their ideas and feelings.

Key Stage 2

Knowledge, skills and understanding

Teaching should ensure that 'investigating and making' includes 'exploring and developing ideas' and 'evaluating and developing work'. 'Knowledge and understanding' should inform this process.

Exploring and developing ideas

Pupils should be taught to:
a. record from experience and imagination, to select and record from first-hand observation and to explore ideas for different purposes
b. question and make thoughtful observations about starting points and select ideas to use in their work
c. collect visual and other information (for example, images, materials) to help them develop their ideas, including using a sketchbook.

Investigating and making art, craft and design

Pupils should be taught to:
a. investigate and combine visual and tactile qualities of materials and processes, and match these qualities to the purpose of the work
b. apply their experience of materials and processes, including drawing, developing their control of tools and techniques
c. use a variety of methods and approaches to communicate observations, ideas and feelings, and to design and make images and artefacts.

Evaluating and developing work

Pupils should be taught to:
a. compare ideas, methods and approaches in their own and others' work and say what they think and feel about them
b. adapt their work according to their views and describe how they might develop it further.

Knowledge and understanding

Pupils should be taught about:
a. visual and tactile elements, including colour, pattern and texture, line and tone, shape, form and space, and how these elements can be combined and organized for different purposes
b. materials and processes used in art, craft and design and how these can be matched to ideas and intentions
c. the roles and purposes of artists, craftspeople and designers working in different times and cultures (for example, Western Europe and the wider world).

Breadth of study

During the Key Stage, pupils should be taught the knowledge, skills and understanding through:

a. exploring a range of starting points for practical work (for example, themselves, their experiences, images, stories, drama, music, natural and made objects and environments)

b. working on their own, and collaborating with others, on projects in two and three dimensions and on different scales

c. using a range of materials and processes, including ICT (for example, painting, collage, printmaking, digital media, textiles, sculpture)

d. investigating art, craft and design in the locality and in a variety of genres, styles and traditions (for example, in original and reproduction form, during visits to museums, galleries and sites, on the internet).

(DfEE QCA 1999, pp. 118–21)

Currently the National Curriculum for Art and Design expresses the idea of process in the first three aspects of the programme of study:

1 Exploring and developing ideas
2 Investigating and making art, craft and design
3 Evaluating and developing work.

It is important to see these strands as an interactive model, not simply as a linear process. For instance, children might start by investigating a range of media and making drawings that they then evaluate in order to go on and develop ideas for a more finished piece of work. Alternatively, they might begin by evaluating the work of an artist, before moving on to exploring other related visual material, developing their own ideas. The programme of study shows that all three aspects are interrelated: 'Teaching should ensure that investigating and making includes exploring and developing ideas and evaluating and developing work' (p. 118).

4 Knowledge and understanding.

The fourth aspect of the programme of study ('Knowledge and understanding') focuses more on the content of children's learning, but it is made clear that this knowledge is not to be acquired for its own sake but should inform the process of investigating and making. Furthermore, although there is a focus on 'visual and tactile elements, including colour, pattern and texture, line and tone, shape, form and space' (ibid., p. 120), there is no implication that these must be learned about in a discrete or sequential way. These elements provide a way of drawing attention to different aspects of our visual and tactile experience, and are the means we use to represent ideas in visual and tactile ways, but they do not exist in isolation from each other. When building an artefact in clay, for example, a child may be thinking more about shape and texture than colour, but these elements cannot be isolated from space, form and pattern. It is the whole that is important, and the 'elements' should be seen in the context of what the child is intending to achieve. Nevertheless, an understanding of the individual elements helps to deepen and enrich both investigation and making.

5 Breadth of study

The 'Breadth of Study' section of the programme of study explains the processes through which the knowledge, skills and understanding are to be taught and, implicitly, how the creative process might be facilitated. Plans for art and design should be developed to allow children to be stimulated by ideas, techniques and materials and other artists' work or cultural traditions. They should provide the opportunity for children to investigate and explore, using a sketchbook at Key Stage 2, in order to create and evaluate their original piece or pieces of practical work. They should allow children to behave both as artists and as critics, investigating and making, talking and thinking. They should encourage children to develop skills in experiencing and reading art and design and cultural artefacts and also to learn how to develop their thinking and communication skills, expressing their ideas and feelings and what they find interesting or significant in their own art work.

Children's experience in art and design should not be limited to the classroom. The internet and the use of interactive whiteboards and data projectors can bring reproductions of the work of other artists into the classroom on a much larger and more representative scale than might have been previously possible, and the use of ICT in this way is encouraged. However, it is no substitute, ultimately, for seeing original work in a real-life setting, whether this is exploring sculpture in public spaces, paintings in museums and galleries or product design in shops. It can be useful to review the variety of places in everyday life where we find 'art and design' in its many forms when thinking about how we can give children first-hand experience of the work of other artists and designers and to aim to include visits to such places in planning for the art and design curriculum.

The QCA schemes of work, which usually provide plans for a half term (or sometimes a term) of weekly lessons linked together by a theme, illustrate how the creative process is interpreted differently in each project. Teachers need to maintain a balance between guiding children through each stage of the creative process and being sensitive to and aware of the life of the project as it unfolds, responding to the needs and discoveries of the children's work as it develops. Different media and processes are highlighted in the QCA plans. For instance, exemplar models of planning sequences for painting projects include 'self-portrait', 'portraying relationships', 'journeys', 'objects and meanings', 'people in action' and a 'sense of place'. These are aimed at specific age ranges, but can usually be easily adapted for older or younger classes. They share the principle (enshrined in the National Curriculum) that children should develop knowledge and understanding of materials and processes, the work of artists, craftspeople and designers, and visual and tactile elements (the elements of colour, shape and pattern are pre-eminent in painting).

Continuity and sequencing of lessons is central to successful learning in art and design. Bruner's (1977) 'spiral curriculum' identifies how sequencing and repetition of critical curriculum components take pupils to greater depth and/or breadth in the subject they are studying. Colour for example, as a thing in itself, is a case in point – one could return to colour time and again to further deepen pupils' knowledge and understanding of it through exploring it from a variety of perspectives, and not, as is often the case, abandoning it once colour wheel exercises have been completed.

In the UK, as teachers build on pupils' experiences gained in the Foundation Stage in Key Stage 1, children will continue to explore creativity through visual, tactile and sensory methods (including play), using a variety of materials and processes. Moving through to Key Stage 2 pupils should continue to learn the required knowledge, skills and understanding in these ways but activities should normally become more complex and refined at this stage. At this stage pupils learn to become more discriminatory in their application and control of materials, tools and techniques. Their critical awareness is raised and challenged to consider the role of art, craft and design in society and in different times and cultures and generally they are becoming stronger as individuals and in what they see, feel and think (DfEE QCA 1999).

ICT and art and design

Many of the most meaningful and rewarding art and design lessons taught in UK primary schools today use ICT in one form or another. Whether locating images of artists' work through a search engine, manipulating photographs using image editing software or simply taking a digital photograph, ICT is an integral part of art and design in the primary school. A study by the Arts Council of England (2003) suggested that appropriate use of ICT in art and design can empower children to become more creative and successful in art and design. But what essentially is it about ICT that can enable children to creatively succeed in art and design? Margaret Talboys tells us that:

> The use of ICT (in art and design) gives opportunities for learning through failure and learning to deal with failure. It provides an archive of decisions taken, a trace, so failure is not so serious and wasteful of time and resources. ICT provides a special place for risk taking where pupils do not feel so open to possible ridicule.
>
> (Becta/QCA 2002. Talboys' submission on investigating how teachers might use ICT to promote pupils' creativity in art and design. March 2002.)

This sums up precisely one of the main features that ICT brings to the subject of art and design, and that is in providing children with opportunities to explore and experiment with a range of possible directions for their work – safe in the knowledge that the 'undo' button is close at hand. In some ways, using art and design software is a natural extension of traditional printmaking techniques. The practices of creating multiple prints or making a number of variations of a particular image are intrinsic aspects of printmaking, and the 'Save as . . . '

facility of many software packages is a digital equivalent, allowing children to experiment with extending their work without the risk of losing or spoiling what they have already created.

Children are often willing to take greater risks with new technologies than most adults. The challenge that faces teachers is to encourage children to channel their enthusiasm for new technologies into creative and constructive activities in the classroom. The opportunity to scan prints – or drawings or paintings, or even photographs of sculptures – onto a computer also offers great potential for the ways in which children can plan and modify their work. For example, a printmaking lesson could be followed by an ICT lesson in which pupils have opportunities to change the colours or even the composition of their prints. Colours and tones can be subtly or dramatically altered, while lines and shapes can be moved around to create new compositions. Prints of these experiments can, in turn, be used as a stimulus for further work in sketchbooks. Many artists would regard experimentation across a range of media as a natural extension of their work – think of how Picasso experimented with paint, print, sculpture and ceramics – and how quickly he would have adapted to the digital age! The role of ICT as a practical process alongside drawing, painting, printmaking, etc. is explored in Chapter 3.

Children's development in art and design

There are numerous stage theories that account for children's cognitive development in education, for example those developed by Erikson (Anselmo and Franz,1995) and Piaget (1976). In art education, however, stage theory is largely associated with the work of Lowenfeld and Brittain (1987). They identified the *scribbling stage (2–4 years)*, followed by the *pre-schematic stage (4–7 years)*, the *schematic stage (7–9 years)* and finally the *gang stage (9–12 years)*. While these stages of development can offer a useful model to teachers in helping them inform their observations of children's work (Green and Mitchell 1997), it has to be noted that psychology has advanced a great deal since and that teachers are no longer satisfied with slotting children into *stages* of the developmental process in the way Lowenfeld and Brittain suggested. Rather, we now accept that things are a great deal more complex and fluid than was once believed, for example, taking account of the need to consider factors relating to other cultures and other ways of seeing. Matthews (1999) and others (e.g. Matthews 2003 and Cox 2005) have challenged the view that the end point of children's development is 'visual realism' – to be skilled in accurate figure drawing, for instance, by the age of 11. They have argued that stage theories are based on this culturally specific and traditional view of visual representation and thus may misrepresent children's development. In any case, it is suggested that children conform only roughly to these stages and any apparent 'stage' of development is best considered without undue emphasis on chronological age (Green and Mitchell 1997).

Bearing this in mind, young children's drawings might sometimes appear to be a series of random marks, which might be seen to fit into the scribbling stage. These early marks engage whole-arm actions, and are often the result of banging and stabbing gestures (Matthews 1997). Referring to these marks as 'scribbling' suggests that they are often considered pre-representational, but research into children's drawings (Matthews 1997; 1999) has led to the conclusion that representational abilities develop at a very early stage and often well before the age of four. Children have a natural interest in the shape, movement and location of objects, and have an innate desire to express emotions and communicate with others through visual representations. What might appear to the adult world as scribbles are in fact, for the child, a map of meaning making; any attempt to interfere in the drawing process should be avoided and any discussion around the child's work should be handled with sensitivity. The one thing to remember is to always listen to what the child says about their drawing (scribbling) and show that you value what they are doing.

As the child progresses, he/she begins to modify and refine shapes or forms and the placement and size of objects or forms are determined according to importance (Green and Mitchell 1997). It is best to ensure that the child experiences a wide range of media, both dry and wet and builds a repertoire or vocabulary of marks which will then enable them to respond in a variety of ways to this developing ability to make marks.

Children's artwork tends to progressively demonstrate closer attention to detail. A base line appears in a landscape for example, and there may also be simultaneous representation of plan and elevation. Matthews (1999) explains that the latter phenomenon is due to the child's attempt to draw directions of movement as a way of indicating three-dimensional qualities. In terms of figure drawing, Cox (1997) observes that as children grow older, they tend to add more features. However, she also remarks that 'In the primary school years, although children may add more items to their figures, they are often reluctant to experiment further, at the same time becoming increasingly dissatisfied with their efforts' (p. 83).

As children become more aware of others' art they can begin to feel particularly self-conscious about their work and their own ability in art and design. It becomes more challenging for teachers to support children as more and more subject knowledge and skill level is demanded. In drawing and painting terms, the base line disappears and depth is represented by a variety of more complex methods, including the overlapping of forms (Green and Mitchell 1997). Matthews (1999) believes that children are unable to overlap objects at an earlier age because this would go against their understanding that objects have uninterrupted boundaries (though this understanding may arguably change as computers and image manipulation programmes such as Photoshop become more widely used by young children). Although some understanding of perspective will be evident, the child may lack understanding of the conventions. This situation is not helped when, as Anning and Ring (2004) state, drawing skills are often left to develop through trial and error. Teacher feedback is sometimes only given infrequently, and often lacks the substance and direction that could make drawing an even more meaningful activity to children.

Transition between Key Stages

Transition from one Key Stage to another, and particularly between the Foundation Stage and Key Stage 1 (KS1), is an issue in art and design as much as it is in other areas of the curriculum, and can be emotionally challenging for young children if it is not handled in a sensitive and thoughtful manner. A recent publication on transition (NFER 2005) found that children had difficulty moving from play-based learning in the Foundation Stage to a more structured curriculum in KS1. The introduction of the literacy and numeracy lessons was identified as 'challenging' and children's skills of independent learning in the Foundation Stage, which were often through the medium of play, were not always built upon in KS1. Yet in art and design play and play-based learning are central to the creative process and to successful art and design, not just at the Foundation Stage but right through the primary phase and beyond and thus could provide children with some continuity during these otherwise disruptive transition periods.

In the Foundation Stage, there is more of a focus on child-initiated activity, whereas in KS1 there is a shift towards more adult-initiated learning. One of the findings of the NFER research (2005) was the negative impact felt by children of too much time spent sitting on the carpet. With changes being made in UK schools in response to the Primary Strategy, it is likely that more flexible approaches to planning will result in more flexibility and greater opportunities for children to be in control of their own activities and learning during KS1 and KS2 as well as in the Foundation Stage. At the same time, teachers do need to ensure, through adult-initiated learning, that at KS1 and beyond the children's repertoire of strategies and skills in a wide range of processes, media and tools is progressively extended.

While building on children's experiences in KS1, teachers in KS2 need to be aware of the further opportunities that will open up in KS3. At KS3 pupils will be expected to develop and improve on their practical and critical skills and to extend their knowledge and experience of materials, processes and practices (DfEE/QCA 1999). Experience of more specialized equipment – such as silk-screen-printing, for example, or the use of sewing machines, can be introduced in KS2.

By KS3 children are at that difficult stage when some will begin to feel self-conscious about their own skill level, particularly in their practical work, and will therefore require a great deal of support from their teachers if they are to continue with art and design beyond KS3. To ease this, a good foundation should be created by giving due attention to art and design during KS2, to develop confidence.

When children arrive at KS3 and enter secondary schooling, often they will find that little consideration is given to their prior art and design experience. Children should therefore be entering the secondary phase with some evidence of past achievements in art and design, which could be in the form of an art portfolio containing, for example, work done during KS2 – sketchbooks are particularly useful here in providing a guide to children's visual development. This portfolio will be helpful both in providing an audit of the child's learning and demonstrating the child's abilities to their new art teacher.

Summary

This chapter has provided an overview of the art and design curriculum and progression in children's learning from the Foundation Stage through to Key Stage 2. The curriculum is continually evolving in response to changing educational priorities and to on-going research. Teachers work in this context and what they do is influenced by it. Crucially, however, the teacher's role is to interact with individual children who are finding their own identity, their own means of understanding and communicating and their own powers of creativity. The structure and content of the curriculum provide a framework for this process and the teacher must be sensitive to the children as people and learners if they are to factilitate their development. Through a rich curriculum and responsive teaching, children should learn more about themselves and their world through art and design as well as learning about art and design.

Bibliography

Anning, A. and Ring, K. (2004), *Making Sense of Children's Drawings*. Buckingham: Open University Press.

Anselmo, S. and Franz, W. (1995), *Early Childhood Development: Prenatal through Age Eight (Second edition)*. Englewood Cliffs, NJ: Prentice Hall.

Arts Council (2003), *Keys to Imagination: ICT in Art Education*. London: Arts Council England.

—— (2006a) 'Artsmark – the arts award for schools', www.artscouncil.org.uk/artsmark, accessed 1 May 2006.

—— (2006b) http://www.creative-partnerships.com/ (accessed 06)

Bruner, J. S. (1977), *The Process of Education*. Cambridge, MA: Harvard University Press.

Cox, M. (1997), *Drawings of People by the Under-Fives*. London: Falmer Press.

Cox, S. (2005), 'Intention and Meaning in Young Children's Drawing', in *International Journal of Art and Design Educatio*n, 24(2): 115–25.

DES (1992), *Art in the National Curriculum (England)*, London: DES/HMSO.

DfEE/QCA (1999), *The National Curriculum: Handbook for Primary Teachers in England – Key Stages 1 and 2*. London: QCA.

DfEE/QCA (2000), *Art and Design – a Scheme of Work for Key Stages 1 and 2* London: QCA.

DfES (2003), *Excellence and Enjoyment: A Strategy for Primary Schools*. London: DfES.

Green, L. and Mitchell, R. (1997), *Art 7–11 Developing Primary Teaching Skills*. London: Routledge.

Harland, J. K., Lord, K. and Stott P. (2000), *Arts Education in Secondary Schools: Effects and Effectiveness*. Slough: NFER.

Herne, S. (2000), 'Breadth and balance? The impact of the National Literacy and Numeracy Strategies on Art in the Primary School' in *International Journal of Art and Design Education* 19(2): 217–23.

Kress, G. (1997), *Before Writing: Rethinking the Paths to Literacy*. London: Routledge.

Lowenfeld, V. and Brittain, L. (1987). *Creative and Mental Growth*. New York: Macmillan.

Macdonald, S. (2004), *The History and Philosophy of Art Education*. Cambridge: Lutterworth Press.

Matthews, J. (1997). 'The 4-dimensional language of infancy: interpersonal basis of art praxis', in *Journal of Art and Design Education*, 16(3): 285–93.

—— (1999), *The Art of Childhood and Adolescence: The Construction of Meaning*. London: Falmer Press.

—— (2003), *Drawing and Painting – Children and Visual Representation (2nd edition)* London: Paul Chapman.

National Advisory Committee on Creative and Cultural Education (NACCCE) (1999), *All Our Futures: Creativity, Culture and Education*. London: DfES.

National Campaign for Drawing, 'Drawing power: the campaign for drawing', www.drawingpower.org.uk, accesed 17 November 2006.

National Foundation for Educational Research (NFER) (Sanders, D., White, G., Burge, B., Sharp, C., Eames, A., McEune, R. and Grayson, H.) (2005), *A Study of the Transition from the Foundation Stage to Key Stage 1*. London: DfES.

National Society for Education in Art and Design (NSEAD) 'Article Title To Go Here', www.nsead.org/addict, accessed 5 May 2006.

Ofsted (2004), *The Annual Report of her Majesty's Chief Inspector of Schools 2003/4* London: DfES/Ofsted.

Piaget, J. (1976), *The Child and Reality*. New York: Penguin Books.

QCA (2005) 'Arts alive: raising attainment across the curriculum'. www.qca.org.uk/artsalive/why_invest/school_imp_attainment.htm accessed 5 May 2006

QCA/DfEE (2000) Curriculum Guidance for the Foundation Stage, London: QCA/DFEE.

Read, H. (1943), *Education Through Art*. London: Faber and Faber.

Talboys, M. (2002) *Investigating How Teachers Might Use ICT to Promote Pupils' Creativity in Art and Design*. London: QCA.

Art and Design Processes

Chapter Outline

Schools teaching the National Curriculum for Art and Design and the Curriculum for the Foundation Stage should ensure that pupils are provided with opportunities to engage in a wide range of art and design processes: these include printmaking, three-dimensional work, textiles, collage and digital media as well as drawing and painting. It is essential that schools that are committed to raising standards for all their pupils should strive towards delivering a broad and balanced curriculum for art and design.

The visual nature of the subject of art and design means that children can quickly develop a sense of their own strengths and weaknesses in relation to those of other children. Whether it is a three-year-old handling paint in the nursery or a ten-year-old manipulating images on a computer, the results of their endeavours are there for all to see. Teachers should be aware of the pressures that some children may consequently feel, and of the impact this may have on their confidence – 'I'll never make a painting as beautiful as hers, so I'm not sure I should even try.'

If, for example, children find observational drawing particularly difficult, then repeated exposure to art lessons that consist of little else are likely to discourage them from pursuing the subject further. The breadth of the curriculum delivered in schools is another issue raised in the 2005 Ofsted subject report:

> Despite examples of excellence, the broad picture for many students is of a curriculum that focuses too narrowly on painting and drawing, so failing to represent the breadth of the subject or present an inclusive approach for learners. Pupils are entitled to experience a range of skills and approaches to art and design, which allow them to develop a personal understanding, realize their potential and be challenged.
>
> (DfEE/QCA 2005, p.4)

There are, perhaps, three reasons why drawing and painting are taught more frequently than other areas of the curriculum: time, space and subject knowledge. First, teachers have limited time to prepare art lessons: specific equipment and resources are needed for three-dimensional work, printmaking or textiles sessions, and when teachers opt to compromise or improvise these lessons can end in disappointment. A printmaking lesson, for example, may require the use of a particular type of polystyrene tile; ceiling tiles bought from a DIY shop are a poor substitute and will be unlikely to result in a successful session, and the resulting crumbling mess will discourage further innovation. Drawing materials, however, need little preparation. They can be cleared away quickly, the finished work requires no special storage arrangements and – last but not least – drawing isn't too messy.

The space available for art activities is also a factor, as few primary schools have dedicated art rooms. A printmaking lesson will place specific demands on the organization of the classroom: tables may need to be rearranged in order that 'inking-up' areas are separated from cleaner areas where work can be left to dry. The construction processes involved in three-dimensional work mean that pupils are unlikely to complete their work within a single session and will need to store it safely between lessons. In contrast, drawing activities are relatively easy to plan and manage: drawing is more suited to whole-class work, with pupils working independently at their desks as they often do in other curriculum areas.

The third reason why drawing and painting are more frequently taught is the level of subject knowledge acquired by teachers and their confidence in teaching it. There is an assumption that pupils already know the basic skills involved in drawing and painting, and that lessons in these areas are about providing opportunities for pupils to refine existing skills rather than to learn new ones. Other areas of the art curriculum require specific techniques to be taught. Those teachers who have received limited guidance in these areas during their initial teacher education courses may be less inclined to choose to teach lessons that require more specific subject knowledge.

Children value the importance of learning new techniques in art and design. Those whose art lessons are restricted to drawing and painting will grow to perceive that progression in art is largely dependent on their ability to draw; those who struggle to develop this ability are likely to lose interest in the subject. This is the key argument for the teaching of a broad art curriculum: if children are to develop their own ideas and decide how they will realize these in their art work, then the wider the range of strategies that are available to them, the better.

This chapter aims to provide teachers with a range of practical information on each of the art and design processes they should teach, from the Foundation Stage through to Key Stage 2. The practical issues and unique qualities of each process are explained, and a selection of examples of pupil work in each of the areas is included. While some processes and activities will appeal to teachers of younger children and others will appeal to those working with older children, teachers should be aware of opportunities for continuity. An activity taught to children in the early years may also appeal to and engage children in Key Stage 2. The materials used may be identical, yet the results be quite different. Whatever the process and whatever the age of the children learning, the emphasis should be upon teaching children to find their own unique way of responding to the challenge of making art.

Drawing

Drawing is hugely important to the intellectual and emotional development of young children and is an essential skill that can support learning across the curriculum. It is not only an aid to invention and imagination, but also an aspect of aesthetic education. It helps children to come to terms with a strange and exciting world by naming it visually. The drawing process can be thought of as a kind of thinking aloud which enables very young children to convey a host of things about their experience of the world that cannot easily be expressed through verbal language – for example shape, proportion and scale. Drawing skills need to be developed systematically and revisited regularly, whatever the eventual focus of the work, and through frequent opportunities to draw, children can learn to observe, analyse, interpret and record what they see and feel.

Drawing has many interrelated functions. It may be used to record the actual appearance of things, communicating perceived reality and engaging children in the problems of making analogies for the things they see. It can be analytical, focusing on selected aspects of the environment and helping children to make sense and order of their surroundings. It may be expressive, imaginative or constructive – a personal response to things seen or imagined. It may be diagrammatic and systemized; it can communicate information to another person, help to solve problems, convey instructions or tell a story.

Drawing processes, strategies and practical considerations

Many non-specialist teachers express concern about teaching drawing on the grounds of their own alleged inability to draw and worry unduly about their ability to demonstrate drawing in front of a class. Such anxieties are largely misplaced – teachers do not need to be proficient at observational drawing in order to help children to draw and demonstrating 'how to draw. . .' something is rarely necessary. Indeed, such demonstrations can lead to children accepting and repeating stereotypical images, rather than looking for their own less sophisticated but more genuine solutions to a challenge. Rather, teachers should help children to explore the properties of materials and the qualities and uses of different drawing tools. It is more important

Figure 3.1 Experiments with line and pattern

that teachers recognize the difficulties that children might encounter than that they themselves demonstrate the solutions to problems.

Of course there are certain core practices in drawing that children need to repeat regularly if their skills are to develop. They need to learn how to hold drawing tools correctly, to explore the range of marks that can be made with them, to experience working on a variety of scales and to develop an awareness of the potential of different materials for future use. Over time, exposure to materials and techniques will enable children to make the informed value judgements which will permit them to match materials to tasks in order to best communicate their ideas. For example, children exploring, on a small scale, the fragility and intricate patterning of a piece of natural coral might choose to draw with fine-line pens or hard pencils, whereas their experience of softer and heavier materials might lead them to choose charcoal, chalk or graphite sticks when making large, expressive drawings of silhouetted trees. For children to be able to make these connections, teachers require some knowledge of the peculiar features of materials, sufficient confidence to allow the child to experiment with them and sympathy with the open-endedness of the art making process. Teachers should think of drawing as a verb not a noun – and see drawing as part of the process of learning, not as a product.

Supporting children's development in drawing

Provide frequent opportunities to experiment with a well-chosen range of drawing materials

There are a great many drawing materials available to schools and it would be easy to be swayed by the glossy pages of the suppliers' brochures and to equate a rich art programme with one offering the widest array of materials. However, exposure to too many materials can sometimes result in children's experiences being superficial. Providing instead a limited range of good-quality materials (see list p. 169), will enable children to explore more thoroughly the properties of each and achieve a greater degree of confidence and control in their handling. Sketchbooks provide the ideal vehicle for this kind of work, allowing children to keep and refer back to their explorations on subsequent occasions. Regular opportunities to experiment with, and develop sensitivity to, drawing materials will allow children to build up a repertoire of skills and knowledge which will ultimately allow them to select with confidence tools appropriate to the task in hand.

Sequence and structure activities so that children can build on their existing skills and discover for themselves how drawing materials work

It is important that children be allowed to learn for themselves. Telling children what different drawing implements will do is no substitute for the sort of experimental mark-making which will allow them to discover how differently an HB pencil performs from a 6B or a fine-line pen from a stick of charcoal. Given time, children will discover for themselves the hard, linear qualities of pens, HB or F pencils, as opposed to the soft, smudginess of chalks or oil pastels. Some drawing tools are easier to control than others, some lend themselves better to exploring texture than line and others work best on a large-scale or on paper with a rougher surface. Teachers should introduce drawing materials selectively and gradually and allow children plenty of time to get to know their characteristics. It is better to link these explorations to specific tasks than to provide one-off exercises out of context, for example experimenting with fine-line pens prior to looking at feathers or trying out smudgy 6B pencils prior to observing furry animals. Children need structured opportunities to experiment, to discover the expressive qualities of drawing media and to make meaningful connections for themselves.

Provide children with opportunities to draw for a variety of purposes; focus on a broad range of subject matter

Different types of drawing develop different knowledge and skills. It is important that children engage in activities that develop not only their observational powers but also their skills of communication, perception, invention and expression. Through well-chosen drawing tasks, children can observe and analyse detail, record and develop their thoughts, tell stories, express and explain their ideas. Most teachers would recognize that a simple starting point from direct observation has potential for promoting learning for children of all ages across the curriculum. It helps them to recognize and appreciate the intrinsic qualities of natural and made objects and leads to a more discriminating understanding of their surroundings. There are an infinite number of starting points and themes for observational drawing. (See suggestions at end of this section.)

The act of translating three-dimensional information into marks on a two-dimensional surface forces the child to look closely and to analyse and is an intensive exercise requiring

Figure 3.2 Observational drawing

considerable concentration. However, working from direct experience is not the only starting point and the National Curriculum for Art and Design requires that children record from first-hand observation, but also from their experience and imagination. Hence they should encounter a broad range of drawing opportunities – free drawing, making maps, pictograms, annotated sketches and diagrams, creating cartoon characters, narrative drawings and story-boards. Equally teachers should ensure that children have opportunities to explore and regularly revisit the visual elements of art – line, tone, shape, texture and pattern – through a range of activities and subject matter chosen for its rich detail. The frequent introduction of artists', illustrators' and designers' work from a range of times and cultures clearly helps to make children aware of the range and purpose of drawing and opens up their eyes to a wealth of possibilities.

Help children to be selective about what they draw

For some children (and adults!) it can be a daunting experience to be confronted with a large and/or complex subject to draw. They are faced with many decisions – where to start, how to fit the whole onto the paper, when to begin focusing on detail, what media to use and so on. Uncertainty about all these factors can serve to inhibit rather than build confidence. Children will often respond more readily if they are given the opportunity to start with just a small area, or to select for themselves the area which interests them most to focus on. For example, with a small but complicated form such as an intricately patterned shell or a gnarled piece of wood an area can be isolated for special attention with a viewfinder – a simple card frame with a small square or rectangle cut out, through which to look. Children can then concentrate on studying pattern or surface texture without being overwhelmed by the object as a whole. The same principle of eliminating confusing detail can be extended to drawing on a larger scale or to working out of doors. Drawing a landscape or a view of a building can be a far less intimidating experience with a viewfinder to help the selection and focus the looking.

Engage children in conversation about their drawing

As in all areas of children's work in art and design, the importance of talk cannot be too strongly emphasized. It is through observing, commenting and careful questioning that teachers can help to increase children's understanding and their vocabulary relating to drawing. Talking about the exploration of materials, the images they are making or any problems they may be encountering, enables children to build up a repertoire of both words and visual ideas.

In a later chapter on planning (Chapter 5) the notion of 'now draw a picture' is introduced, along with an entirely justified health warning. The example highlights the differences between the unsupported drawing solicited by a teacher as an illustrative adjunct to a piece of writing towards the end of a child's Literacy session, and the properly structured and guided observational drawing lesson delivered by the same teacher later in the day. The most significant difference between the two activities will almost certainly be the degree of ongoing constructive comment about the children's work in the latter case – the use of rich, descriptive language and salient questioning, which will keep alive their enthusiasm for the task and enable them to reflect on and refine their work as it progresses. For example, in observing the intricate markings on a shell, thoughtful questioning can help to focus looking and can help children to make decisions about the use and appropriateness of materials: Where is the darkest/lightest part? Which part curves the most? Are all those lines the same? What will you use to draw those very jagged parts? What else could you add to . . .? Where will you need to use your smudgy pencil? etc. Encouraging children to share in each other's discoveries and to reflect and conjecture about their work is an integral part of the learning process. There is, clearly, a correlation between the quality of children's artwork and the quality of the language and discussion that initiates, supports and follows it.

Organization for drawing

1 *Whole-class or group work?* Much depends on the scale of the work and the availability of materials. Whereas some aspects of art and design are very messy and/or organizationally complex, there is no reason why drawing should not be carried out as a whole-class activity. So long as there are adequate materials and space, it makes sense for the teacher to be able to model processes and skills and share ideas with the whole class at once, while also interacting with individuals.

2 *Organization and storage of materials* Materials and equipment for drawing should be clearly labelled and graded where appropriate, e.g. HB, 3B, 6B and aquarelle pencils. Materials that are most frequently used should be set out at a convenient level (colour-coded storage trays or containers are most useful) so that they are easily accessible. Those less frequently used can be stored at higher or lower levels. Some schools make up special 'drawing boxes' for use by the children, containing a basic selection of hard and soft drawing materials – two or three different pens, pencils ranging between HB to 6B, charcoal, pastels and pen and ink.

Practical activities

Box 3.1 Some suggested starting points for observational drawing . . .

1 *natural forms*: plants, shells, bones, grasses, feathers, etc.;
2 *made objects*: old tools, bits of machinery, buildings, street furniture, broken machine parts, shoes, kitchen utensils, bicycles, dolls, bottles, decorative fabrics;
3 *inside/outside:* sections cut through fruit and vegetables e.g. pomegranates, cabbages, insides of old clocks and watches, broken shells, etc.;
4 *groups of objects*: bunches of keys, collection of spanners, small toys;
5 *reflective or distorted surfaces*: spoons, shiny kettles, concave or convex mirrors, glass, magnifying lenses, tin foil;
6 *comparisons and contrasts:* rough and smooth objects, large and small, regular and irregular, objects scaled up or down, seen from unusual angles, etc.

Box 3.2 Some suggested starting points for imaginative drawing . . .

1 *favourite places:* the circus, funfair, zoo or swimming pool and clowns, trapeze artists, animals, dancers, swimmers, lion tamers and acrobats;
2 *toys and machines*: designs, adaptations of favourites, futuristic inventions;
3 *a family event*: a party or picnic, a day at the seaside, a wedding;
4 *palaces, castles and fantasy homes*: houses and gardens of the past, present and future;
5 *characters from a story:* made up, remembered or adapted;
6 *special celebrations:* birthdays, carnivals, christenings, Divali, Christmas – customs and costumes;
7 *me and my friends:* in a variety of real and imaginary situations, at work and at play;
8 *journeys and transport:* holidays, postcards of places real or imagined, aeroplanes and spaceships, submarines and speedboats, bicycles and buses.

Painting

Painting is almost synonymous with colour: when we think of painting we think of colour, when we think of colour we think of painting. Colour can be a great source of enjoyment and provides a powerful language to express responses to the world. Young children need to experience colour in a wide range of media to become sensitive to its expressive qualities and to be able to recognize and name each colour in its many variations in the environment. Through working with colour and paint, children can develop practical, organizational and creative skills and develop a repertoire of representational concepts. Colour and paint allow for the creation of unique meaning unavailable in quite the same way in any other medium.

When teaching painting it is important to balance opportunities to develop skills, including careful demonstrations of techniques, with more open creative sessions to allow children to follow their own lines of discovery and to respond to their inner motivations at their own pace. Painting can be a tool for learning and, as one of the most accessible practices of the arts, it can also play a powerful role in the development of individuality and identity. Teaching children to paint involves encouraging an intuitive and experimental approach, one that values the flow of expression and visual communication. Painting can have a therapeutic effect: this perhaps stems from the focusing required when the hand, eye and brain are fully engaged, the creative flow and the potential for authentic, individual expression. In this section you will find a range of useful practical information on paint systems and the types of paint used by young children, as well as some reflections on approaches to teaching painting at the Foundation Stage and across Key Stages 1 and 2.

Learning to see is a fundamental reason for art making activities, and gaining an appreciation and sensitivity towards colour is an essential element of an individual's broad and balanced art education. This means that children develop a sharpened visual sense, an ability to perceive with greater insight, an attention to detail and an awareness of the innate characteristics and expressive qualities of the things around them. There are many activities that can support this process but responding to direct experience and colour mixing from close observation are recognized as activities that, with regular practice, make a significant contribution. Painting can help to develop children's capacity for prolonged concentration and provide a depth of visual experience that aids memory, prompts questioning, discussion, language and conceptual development and forms the basis for personal expression.

Painting: processes, strategies and practical considerations

Children will have had varying experiences of painting, even before beginning the Foundation Stage, and it is important that teachers should be aware of a range of practical issues that will support children's learning in this key area.

Box 3.3 Key considerations

1 From the early years onwards, the foundations are being laid for understanding colour; encouraging children to experiment will build their confidence and enhance their enjoyment.

2 Children will experience colour differentiation through early 'free painting' with fingers and with brushes at the easel, rather than on tables, where they may have difficulty reaching the top of their paper.

3 The paint young children use should be thick enough so that it does not run (although some early years specialists advise the provision of a water pot to introduce the experience of varied consistency).

4 From an early age, involve children in mixing liquid paint from powder (the addition of a small amount of washing-up liquid will improve the consistency of the paint and ease the mixing process).

5 Opportunities should be provided to explore warm and cool colours, colour related to mood and colour related to immediate experiences, for example, weather and seasons.

6 Once children have acquired basic skills and understanding they should be introduced to more sophisticated paint systems, e.g. the 'double primary' system.

7 Block paints cannot be shared (mixing paints takes place on top of the blocks). Try to ensure children have plenty of room and that they sit or stand 'square ' to the paper.

Paint systems

In the early years it is appropriate for children to experiment with mixing and matching colour from observation, building on the earlier mixing experimentation and experience. At this stage a paint system is required which provides the opportunity to work with a range of colours, providing the full potential for mixing all colours in subtle shades. Best practice is often achieved when a teacher, or better still a whole school, adopts a standardized paint system and range of colours as basic equipment in each classroom. This will almost certainly be a form of tempera paint: powder, blocks or ready-mixed paint using what has become known as the 'double primary' system of colours. This can be extended by the use of watercolour boxes for small-scale work and painting outside the classroom.

Box 3.4 Key colour systems

1   Primary colours (red, yellow and blue) – these are pure colours that cannot be mixed from other pigments. Teachers should be aware that Key Stage 2 children may be learning about light in Science and that red, blue and *green* are the three 'light primary' colours – and these combine to make white light.

2   Secondary colours (orange, green and purple) – these can each be mixed from two primary colours completing the six-part colour circle.

3   The addition of white allows us to mix 'tints', and black 'shades'. (Remember that 'paint primaries' are *subtractive*, while 'light primaries' – red, green and blue – are *additive*.)

4   Colour families – colours which are close to each other on the colour circle 'harmonize' and give us a 'colour family' (e.g. cool blues and greens).

5   Complementary colours – Colours opposite each other contrast and are called 'complementary' colours (e.g. red and green, blue and orange, yellow and violet). Artists and designers have found that a small amount of a complementary colour brings its opposite to life when they are placed next to each other. A complementary colour can also be used to reduce the intensity of its opposite when mixing.

We have already identified the principle that children should have access to quality art materials and that it is better to have a small quantity of *good*, relatively inexpensive materials than a lots of cheap, *poor* materials that may lead to disappointment and lack of success. Unfortunately the suppliers of paints tend to provide what sells, so it can sometimes be difficult to obtain the colours recommended in the double primary system. Many 'special offers' include green and browns, which are not necessary and encourage children to go for superficial, ready-made solutions.

Tempera paint is the most widely used paint in schools and is intended to be used as an opaque paint: in other words, it should be mixed thick enough to obliterate the colour of the paper it is used on.

Watercolour, on the other hand, has a much finer pigment and is designed to be used in thin transparent washes on white paper. Each art educationalist has his or her preferred type of paint that they will recommend with well argued justification, but all three forms of paint are capable of excellent results if used in appropriate ways.

Theoretically all colours should be able to be mixed from the primary colours plus white but, because pigments are not pure, this does not work well in practice. The double primary colour system has been developed as the most limited set of colours which will truly provide the full range of colour mixing possibilities. It is more important to standardize the range of colours available than the type of paint medium. The system uses a warm and cool version of each of the primary colours (i.e. brilliant blue, turquoise, crimson, vermillion, brilliant yellow, lemon yellow), together with black and white.

Variations: Some do not automatically include black, due to the tendency of some children to outline and mix darker shades using black alone. The turquoise can be replaced by Prussian blue which will produce a range of blacks when mixed with vermilion. Alternatively, black can be replaced by Prussian blue as a third blue. Recipes can be developed for various colours. 'Pure' primaries can be mixed from equal quantities of the warm and cold versions of the primary colour. 'Pure' secondaries are mixed from appropriate primaries:

> orange – brilliant yellow and vermilion
> green – lemon yellow and turquoise
> violet – crimson, brilliant blue (and a touch of white).

When mixing and matching from observation, teachers and children can share their experimentation and research. A wide range of greens can be obtained by cross-mixing all the blues and yellows, and by adding small amounts of red – the complementary of green. Colours can also be extended into pastel tints with white and shades with black. A wide range of browns can be obtained mixing blues with vermilion, and extended by adding brilliant yellow. 'Colour greys' and 'tertiary colours' are the technical titles used for the many subtle colours made from various proportions of all the primaries.

There are essentially three different paints available for use in schools – powder colour, tempera blocks (watercolour) and ready-mixed paint. All provide good educational experience and have advantages and disadvantages.

Powder colour

Powder colour is the cheapest form of paint. It can be mixed to a variety of consistencies and also be used to cover large areas for mural and theatrical scale work. It requires preparation and can be quite messy which can be off-putting to some teachers. Some argue that the process of mixing from a dry powder is fundamental, while others maintain it distracts the learner from an immediacy of a response to colour. Powder colour mixes easily to produce a thick consistency and the dry powder can be picked up with a wet brush to adjust mixing in progress. It is stored in trays with individual containers and used with a mixing palette (and, like all painting systems, plenty of clean water!). Trays require regular topping up with new supplies of powder colour and can be messy when accidentally dropped!

Tempera blocks

Blocks are slightly more expensive than powder paints, but are more economical in use than ready-mixed. They are perhaps the most accessible and most economical in preparation time and the least problematic in terms of classroom organization, storage and use. This is an important factor, as children can be encouraged to take more responsibility for their organization. However, if not washed properly and maintained they can become dispiritingly unattractive! They are also not suitable for large-scale work and require the acquisition of specific mixing skills to become effective.

New tempera blocks should be stuck into eight-welled palettes with PVA glue. They are easy to stack and store and provided they are cleaned and drained after use, instantly accessible.

They can be more difficult to mix to a thick consistency unless wetted before use, allowing time for the top surface of the block to soften up. Mixing is done in patches on top of the blocks themselves using a stiff brush and avoiding concentration in the centre of the block that will inevitably wear a hole in the centre. When a block is nearly finished, the section of the palette should be filled with water and left to soak overnight. In the morning the remains will be soft and can be removed with a knife and stiff washing-up brush and replaced.

Ready-mixed paints

Ready-mixed paint can be used in much the same way as powder colour can, and as a liquid paint it provides exceptional fluency of use. However, it has its drawbacks: it cannot be thickened as it is already liquid; the dispensation of paint requires supervision and takes time, and it is slightly more expensive. Some argue it is also more wasteful as any paint left in palettes at the end of a lesson has to be washed away, although it can be stored in separate little pots and a little water added the following day.

Ready-mixed paints should be set out in palettes in small quantities at the beginning of a painting session and need little or no water to mix to a painting consistency. The plastic bottles are best stored horizontally and need to be shaken from time to time as the liquid binder separates out from the pigment over time. The little plastic tops must be carefully replaced after use, as when left open dry paint causes blockages in the nozzle which can result in messy accidents when bottles are squeezed!

The best paint?

Perhaps the two most important factors in choosing the paint system are first, an existing school policy, and second, your own skills and understanding. If you can use one of the types of paint successfully yourself, you will be able, with a little self analysis and consideration about the age and experience of the children, to break down the skills and concepts you have acquired and successfully demonstrate and coach the children at an appropriate level.

Strategies for implementing a standardized paint system

Clearly as an individual class teacher you can implement a system in your own classroom, and if you are the subject leader for art you should endeavour to convince your colleagues of its value. Whichever system you choose, be aware that it can be expensive so may have to be implemented in a phased programme. As it is more important to standardize colour than paint type it is a good idea to make sure all future orders are only for the double primary colour system. Make an audit of the colours you have which you can use. The first order you make can concentrate on the colours you don't have. (Remember you will need to order twice as much yellow and white as other colours as they get used up more quickly.) Advise children to add dark colours to light, rather than the other way around. This saves overuse of white and yellow. Blocks and powder colour will need the appropriate eight-section palettes. Most palettes are suitable for ready-mixed paint. Remove all non-standard colours.

Box 3.5 Skills to develop in painting at the Foundation Stage

1 Use powder, ready-mixed, large watercolour blocks, finger paints.
2 Use a range of tools: brushes, sponges, rollers, different papers and surfaces.
3 Scribble with paint, cover paper with areas of paint.
4 Use paint to express feelings, record events and develop imagination.
5 Develop techniques: mixing paint, controlling paint.
6 Choose brushes and equipment.
7 Name primary colours.
8 Describe colours, e.g. red like a pillar box.

Box 3.6 Skills to develop in painting at Key Stage 1

1 Identify and mix primary and secondary colours.
2 Use brushes and paint to make a range of marks on paper.
3 Begin to consider composition.
4 Make both imaginative and observational paintings.
5 Control the amount of water added to paint.
6 Notice and describe texture.
7 Select appropriate brushes and choose size/colour of paper.
8 Choose brushes and equipment.
9 Describe colours, e.g. red like a pillar box.

Box 3.7 Skills to develop in painting at Key Stage 2

Developing the language of colour

Primary colours are red, yellow and blue.

Secondary colours are mixtures of two primaries – green, purple and orange.

Tertiary colours are mixtures of secondaries.

Each primary colour has a complementary colour made from the other two primaries :

red/green   blue/orange   yellow/purple

Name and describe colours beyond the primaries – e.g.vermilion is an orange-red, crimson is a blue-red, turquoise is a green-blue.

Describe the qualities of colour:

tone (light/dark)   pigment (opaque/translucent)

surface (shiny/matt)   temperature (cool/warm)

Consider ways in which colour might be used to express mood and feelings.

Organization for painting

1 A central tray of powder colours or dispensed, ready-mixed paint can be shared if within easy reach, although children will benefit from having their own set.

2 To encourage mixing, all pupils should have their own palettes, brushes and water. (Some art educators even suggest having two pots of water if possible – one to clean the brush and a second for clean water for mixing!)

3 A small square of J-cloth or sponge is useful to wipe or blot the brush although children can learn to control the wetness of the brush by wiping it against the side of the water pot.

4 Much of the time the primary colours, plus white, should be available and other colours can be added to extend experience. At other times resricting the number of colours available to two will encourage further experimentation.

5 Remember to provide children with a choice of scales on which to work – the most disappointing displays of children's artwork are those that feature 30 pieces of identical size.

6 Newspaper can be used to protect tables – but this is of questionable value as they will still need to be sponged. Although it can help to mop-up spilt water, observation reveals that newspaper can also become a nuisance and can complicate the table set up.

7 Have plenty of cheap decorators' sponges available. Plain, coloured, plastic tablecloths can protect tables from all types of practical work, but care must be taken when working with craft knives.

8 Mixing paint with PVA glue and other additives such as sand, sawdust, etc. can extend the variety of experience. It is best to use recycled food containers for this kind of work as the PVA can stain and spoil water pots and pallets if allowed to dry. PVA glue used on top of block paints will 'seal' the paint if allowed to dry and is not recommended!

Practical activities

Painting can be used to explore abstract shape, colour and pattern: for instance, children could investigate primary colours or geometric structures through studying paintings by Mondrian, Klee or Kandinsky. Inspiration can also be taken from art, design and pattern in a wide range of artforms and cultural practices, for example the bright colours and complementary contrast of Guatemalan embroidery or the geometric shapes and symbols in African basketry. Pattern work can draw on tessellation or reinforce shape concepts in the early years. There is a wealth of visual resources to be found in contemporary wrapping papers and everyday textiles.

Classroom projects might explore the origins of painting, for instance, cave painting using natural pigments; or later styles such as Impressionism, where children could have opportunities to study the effects of light, weather and atmosphere on colour. Pointillism, where dots of pure colour are combined to create complex surfaces, can provide inspiration for practical work, while other approaches could include exploring the use of Matisse's flat decorative colour or the exaggerated, expressionist colour of the Fauvists. Opportunities exist across the curriculum to paint what can be seen and investigated whether through close observation, collections of objects (perhaps arranged as a 'still life'), interiors, the local environment or

Figure 3.3 Spin painting

Figure 3.4 *(below)* Watercolour inspired by Patrick Heron paintings

landscape. Finally, painting, like written language, can be a vehicle for recording experience using memory or relating experience in new and unusual combinations.

Box 3.8 Painting activity ideas

1 Marble rolling – roll paint-covered marbles around a shoebox lined with paper, exploring ideas of controlled marks and random marks – *see Jackson Pollock.*
2 Make a large-scale group painting based on outlines of body shapes by taking turns to lie on the paper (in an 'action' pose) while each body shape is drawn around, overlapped, etc. – *see Yves Klein.*
3 Experiment with warm and cool colours – take a cool landscape and make it warm – or take a warm landscape and make it cool! – *see Monet, Whistler.*
4 Laminate a collection of random shapes that children have drawn and cut out from card; use these shapes as the basis for abstract compositions by overlapping and interlocking them and drawing around them *see Paul Klee.*
5 'Is my blue the same as your blue?' – Make a collection of blue objects, illustrating the range of hues and tones within a single colour – *see Tony Cragg.*
6 Use aerial photographs as the inspiration for abstract paintings – roads and rivers could form lines, children can try to match the textures of the land within the shapes – *see Patrick Heron.*

Printmaking

There is something slightly magical about the process of printmaking. Whether it is the careful carving of lines into a sheet of polyboard, or the spontaneity of using leftover paint to make a monoprint on a table, making a print is a rewarding experience. Many teachers, and their pupils, will find that printmaking – the process of transferring an image from an object to paper – is one of the most exciting, fulfilling and challenging areas of the art and design curriculum.

However, printmaking can also be frustrating, confusing and messy. A teacher who starts the day with a bag of potatoes, some tubes of ink and the best of intentions can easily end it resolving to avoid printmaking for the rest of their career. This section outlines the practical issues teachers will need to consider when planning to teach printmaking. It suggests some reasons why printmaking is a valuable experience for children and provides details of a range of print processes used in the primary classroom and at the Foundation Stage.

While all teachers of children aged 3–11 are almost certain to teach drawing and painting, those who engage their pupils in printmaking lessons are demonstrating a more adventurous approach to their art teaching and are showing that they have a commitment to teaching the art and design curriculum. Printmaking can be challenging – but if teachers and their pupils are able to manage its practicalities then they will also experience its rewards.

Why make prints?

There are several reasons for making prints: some aesthetic, some theoretical, and some practical. The most obvious, practical reason for printmaking is that the process enables us to make multiple copies of an image. This is one reason why artists make limited edition prints and why prints are typically sold for less money than paintings. While your pupils, however talented, may struggle to find a thriving market for selling their work, having several copies of their print means that they are able to swap pictures with their friends, or compile their efforts into a class book.

Making multiple copies also offers children opportunities to experiment with their work without risking failure. Planning a print with several layers of colour, for example, can be confusing. If a number of copies of the print are made at each stage, it is possible to 'return' to a previous stage if necessary (a little like the 'undo' function on a computer package). Making multiple copies also offers teachers an opportunity to compile a portfolio of pupils' prints – a useful resource and record of pupil achievement.

Other reasons for making prints are aesthetic. Printmaking processes encourage children to broaden the visual vocabulary of the marks they make, marks that are often distinct from those made by drawing or painting. When we make a print we have only a limited amount of control over the way ink is transferred to paper and the resulting marks can surprise us. Sometimes the accidental and unexpected marks turn out to be those that are most essential to the work: when one layer of ink is applied over another, for example, some of the first colour will show through, creating unexpectedly rich textures. A successful print is often a combination of the intentional and the unintentional.

Finally, printmaking offers opportunities for children to reflect on the progression of their work. A child making a painting easily becomes immersed in the physicality of the process, absorbed by the way paint leaves the brush and changes the image. Younger children's engagement with this process is more important than the product that emerges from it: they literally don't know when to stop. A beautiful composition can swiftly become obscured by subsequent layers of paint. As children grow older, however, they should learn to pause and review the progress of their work. The sequence of operations involved in many printmaking processes allows and encourages them to do this, as one stage needs to be completed before the next is begun: for example, one layer of ink needs to dry before a second is added. Children should be encouraged to ask themselves questions: Is it finished? If not, then why not? What is missing in the work? These are the same questions that artists ask of themselves and their work, questions that can prompt and encourage reflection on the process of making art.

Printmaking: processes, strategies and practical considerations

Printmaking processes begin with patterns of footprints from puddles and extend to traditional techniques such as etching and lithography and modern innovations such as the digital manipulation of photographs. Within each process there is room for creativity and individuality. But, more so than with drawing or painting, there are rules – some 'do's and 'don't's – that children need to follow if their experiences in printmaking are to be enjoyable rather than frustrating. The processes can be divided into four areas:

1 relief prints (additive method) – the print surface is constructed from materials then inked up and printed
2 relief prints (subtractive method) – lines or sections of a tile or object are removed, ink is applied to the remaining tile and printed
3 monoprints – paper placed over ink that has been applied to a level surface; each print is unique
4 rubbings – use crayons to create patterns on paper placed on textured surfaces

Relief prints (additive method)

Handprints

Handprints could rightly be regarded as page one of the printmaking book – a simple activity accessible to all children. As with any process, however, the only limits are those of your pupils' imagination. Encourage them to experiment with overlapping prints, prints grouped together to form larger shapes, patterns or images. (It is interesting to reflect on the fact that even this simple process can be developed to a high level of sophistication. Artist Marcus Harvey's 'Myra' caused controversy when exhibited at the Royal Academy of Arts in 1997 – the portrait of murderer Myra Hindley was composed entirely of handprints, each taken from a mould of a child's hand.)

Found objects

Making prints using found objects can be both surprising and rewarding. A particular pattern or texture of an object might easily be overlooked, until it is inked up and pressed onto paper. Even with this relatively straightforward activity, take care to vary the amount of ink that is applied to a textured object. Too little will mean the print will be only partly visible, too much and the detail that makes an object an interesting choice will be lost.

Card/string prints – collographs

Making prints by rolling ink across lengths of string glued to card is an initially sticky but ultimately satisfactory way to introduce children to printmaking. Problems occur when children attempt to apply glue to the string rather than the board. A thin coat of PVA should be spread across the card, the string arranged and carefully pressed into the glue. When the glue is dry – it will be transparent – ink can be rolled across and paper placed on top to make the print. (A useful drawing activity to precede this process would be to make drawings using a single, continuous line.) String prints can be developed to make collographs – pieces of card, fabric or other textured material can be stuck to card, inked up and printed.

Relief prints (subtractive method)

Potato prints

Few teachers can claim to have approached their first potato-print lesson with a spring in their step and a song in their hearts! However, prepare to be surprised by the range of results that can be achieved with the simplest of ingredients. Put simply – and there isn't really another way of describing it – most potato prints are made by cutting a potato in half, placing one half into ink and then pressing it down onto paper. But we should encourage children to explore the possibilities of this medium as with any other, even a simple process can produce a wide range of outcomes. Experiment, for example, with different papers, different vegetables, overlapping prints, applying ink or paint carefully with a small paintbrush. You will be surprised at the range of possible outcomes.

The success of your prints will be dependent partly upon making creative connections – between, for example, the shape of the potato and that of another object – and partly upon 'thinking sideways' – recognising, for example, that it need not always be the cut face of the potato that is inked up. Two tips: avoid substituting paint for ink, and try picking up the paper and pressing it into the potato rather than pressing the potato down on to the paper.

Press prints

Press printing is a form of block printing using sheets of polystyrene board, or polyboard. Block prints can also be made from wood or lino (although any reluctance on the part of the teacher to invest in the collection of sharp tools required to cut these materials is entirely reasonable!). Though polyboard is less durable than wood or lino – it is inclined to fragment when cut into complex shapes – it is cheaper, and pencils or biros can be used to carve lines into it.

The principle of press printing is basically similar to making potato prints, but a little more explanation is required, particularly if you want your pupils to experiment with multiple colours. Begin by planning a design on paper; sketch the drawing lightly onto the polyboard (tracing and transferring is too complicated) and carve the lines deeply enough to be easily visible but not so deep that the tile disintegrates. Mix two colours of ink (a single primary colour straight from the tube can be a little overpowering) across the top of a palette wide enough to accommodate a roller (A perspex sheet or a vinyl floor tile can also be used as an inking plate). Roll the ink out until its consistency changes slightly to become smooth and even (to begin with it will be quite tacky); ensure that the roller is covered in a thin, even layer of ink by lifting and spinning it slightly before

Figure 3.5 Press print with repeat pattern

rolling again. Carry the same motion across to your polyboard tile, ensuring that you cover it to the corners. Note that it is better to build up the ink on the tile by adding several thin layers of ink rather than attempting to apply one thick layer.

A common mistake is to start with too much ink on the inking plate, which means that the roller does not roll effectively, but slides, and the ink is not evenly applied to the tile. If the ink is applied too thickly, the ink will fill in the grooves you have made and the print will lose definition. Move the tile to a clean table and place your paper squarely over the top, leaving a large border. Apply pressure by smoothing over the paper with one hand while holding it in place with the other. Alternatively use a suitable burnishing tool, such as a smooth pebble or the back of a wooden spoon to provide more pressure. It is suggested that you should make three or four copies of your print at this stage. This will provide you with opportunities to experiment with each print in a different way, while still having an original to return to.

Encourage children to reflect on their composition to decide which areas they want to keep in the existing colour. They should then remove these areas from their tile before adding a second, and possibly third, layer of colour. Two or three tones of the same colour can be an effective combination (as well as a practical solution to the problem of limited resources in the classroom). There are various options for extending this activity. Complex patterns can be made by designing a tile that, when printed repeatedly, forms a continuous pattern (links can be made with work by William Morris) or by cutting tiles into a range of tessellating shapes.

Monoprints

Most print processes are developed in order to facilitate the printing of multiple copies of an image. Each monoprint however, as the term suggests, is individual, and can be made in one of two ways. Younger children can experiment with paint mixed with shaving foam, or commercially produced finger paints, and spread directly onto tables. Shapes can be drawn into the foam or paint with their fingers, before placing paper over the top and printing. Success is not guaranteed, but each print takes only a few seconds! This technique can be developed with older children, who can roll ink – or apply paint – onto a flat surface such as plastic or Perspex, then place paper over the top, smoothing it out to pick up the subtler marks.

A second technique for monoprinting involves rolling out a very thin, almost dry layer of ink, then placing a sheet of paper carefully over it and drawing on the back of the paper. Experiment with a range of drawing materials, from hard pencils to soft crayons – each will print the same colour but with contrasting textures. Any contact with the back of the

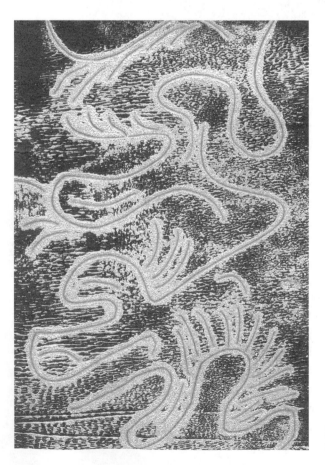

Figure 3.6 Monoprint – light ink on dark background

paper will result in fingerprints being added to your print, so try to avoid accidentally touching the surface with your fingers – unless, of course, fingerprints are part of the design . . . . With either of these approaches to monoprinting, the beauty of the print often lies in the spontaneous splashes and textures created by ink – whether intentional or otherwise.

Rubbings

Make a collection of natural or manufactured materials and use wax crayons on thin sheets of paper – newsprint is ideal – to make rubbings of the textures. Cheap, large wax crayons are ideal because of their durability, although the range of colours is slightly unpleasant. Encourage children to experiment with mixing two or three colours together by overlapping them on the same rubbing. Rubbings can be used to create further work in different ways, for instance they can be torn or cut into shapes and collaged together, or a watercolour wash can be added to bring out the rubbing through the process of 'wax resist' (the wax crayon resists the watercolour).

Organization for printmaking

Planning:

1 Planning weekly sessions means that there will be time for prints to dry; this is useful when several colours are applied to the same print.
2 Whole-class activity or groups only? Your strategy for organizing a printmaking lesson depends very much upon you as a teacher – and your pupils! While there is no rule that states that printmaking should only be taught to one group of children at a time, teaching printmaking to a whole class does demand a fairly high level of organizational skill. Beginning teachers would be advised to restrict themselves to teaching printmaking to groups in order to provide children with the support that they may need. A whole-class session may be harder to manage, but it enables a stronger focus on the process (allocate each table a different activity – have separate tables for drawing, cutting, inking and printing). Group work is easier to manage – but there may be some danger that the art activity becomes marginalized as other subjects demand teacher attention.

Classroom organization

1 Drying racks are essential for printmaking – remind children to fill the rack up from the bottom to the top.
2 Washing lines, hung with drying prints, are not only practical, but also look great – an energetic indication of work in progress.
3 *Always* use water-based ink, as oil-based inks make permanent stains and need to be cleaned from equipment with solvents, which must not be used by children.

Intervention

1 Remember to offer children choices – for example, of scale on which to work, and of colours to use.
2 Mix colours – don't use straight from the tube unless you positively want a primary colour. Printmaking inks are often particularly vibrant colours. Remember to apply lessons learned in painting: a bright green, for example, can be 'mixed down' with a little red – its complementary colour – to make it a more natural, leaf-like hue.
3 When teaching children how to make multicoloured prints, begin with abstract designs where the placing of a particular colour in a particular place is less crucial.
4 If you don't want any white areas within your press print (presuming that you are printing onto white paper), begin by inking up the polyboard and making several prints with one flat area of colour before removing any parts of the tile.
5 You might choose to teach your children the rule that lighter colours should be applied to a print before darker colours are applied on top. (Close study of Picasso's linocuts, however, will reveal that he sometimes began by applying black, then brown, then finally yellow. The message here is that, having learned the rules, try breaking them!)
6 Remember that the image you draw or assemble will be reversed in your print. If you want pupils to include text or letters, make drawing them in reverse part of the lesson.

Why has my print turned out like this?

Practise print processes yourself – making mistakes is good, you'll be putting yourself in the place of the learner and consequently will learn more!

Some of the detail of the child's design has been lost because . . .

1 there was too much/little ink on the tile;
2 they didn't apply sufficient pressure;
3 they didn't apply pressure evenly;
4 the ink was too dry/wet;
5 the paper was too thick;
6 they didn't carve your lines deeply enough;
7 they were over-ambitious and included too much detail in the first place!

The colours are very bright and clash with one another.
. . . Mix down primary colours with complementary colours.

The colours are muddy.
. . . You didn't wait for the first layer of ink to dry before you applied the second.

The writing on the print doesn't make sense.
. . . You forgot to reverse letters and numbers!

Practical activities

Foundation Stage
Hand/finger/footprints
Printing with made and natural objects
Fruit/vegetable printing (without making incisions)
Rubbings of textures

Key Stage 1
Potato prints – cutting into the surface with pencils
One or two-colour press prints (polystyrene board)
String and card prints
Monoprints – painting ink onto tables
Use art and design software to create repeated reflected/rotated patterns

Key Stage 2
Multicoloured press prints
Experiments with repeat patterns, rotating patterns, etc.
Monoprints – rolling a thin layer of ink onto a palette, placing paper over and drawing on the back with a range of tools
Scanning prints onto a PC and manipulating them using art and design software

Sculpture

Sculpture provides unique visual, formal and tactile languages through which children can explore ideas, impulses and feelings, develop their creativity and imagination, engage with aesthetic experiences and construct meanings.

Form is the pre-eminent element in sculpture. In terms of art generally, the word can refer to all the characteristics of an object or artefact. In sculpture it specifically refers to three-dimensional properties (while shape is two dimensional). In three-dimensional art, form can be created directly in malleable clay or construction materials whereas in two-dimensional art, form is represented through illusion on a flat surface. There is a wealth of art and culture from which to explore sculptural form, from the simplified and powerful expressive forms of African sculptures, to Henry Moore's imposing figures; from the classic perfection of Michelangelo's sculpture to Kiki Smith's representations of human form; from the smooth elegance of Brancusi's bronzes to the natural materials of Andy Goldsworthy's ephemeral works constructed from found natural materials.

It is worth spending some time analysing what practices should be included under the heading of sculpture so that children might be introduced to a range of appropriate examples, concepts, vocabulary, materials, skills and techniques and ways of working.

At the Foundation Stage, children should be introduced to a range of materials that can be used to make three-dimensional work. Many of these materials will be familiar to them in different contexts: cardboard cereal packets and plastic bottles may have almost assumed clichéd roles in the creative work of young children, but providing children with opportunities to use such familiar, everyday objects in different contexts can subtly alert them to the particular structural, practical or aesthetic qualities they have to offer. By encouraging children to engage in the process of transforming these objects through combining them, joining them and changing them, early years practitioners can provide experiences that heighten children's awareness and appreciation of the visual and tactile similarities and connections between objects that are otherwise unrelated. An empty plastic bottle quickly ceases to be a item of rubbish when it is picked up, covered in papier mâché, painted and launched as a rocket, while the range of possibilities offered by an egg box is almost endless. Perhaps it was this process of recognition and regeneration that Picasso was referring to when he talked about his yearning to produce art that could have been made by a child: many of his sculptures – a toy car transformed into a monkey's head, for example – demonstrate that he valued that process of making connections between objects that are unrelated save for their unexpected visual parallels.

There are three broad areas of 3D work that are common in Key Stages 1 and 2:

- *plastic materials* – Plasticine, dough, and clay;
- work with *'rigid' or 'resistant' materials* – carving soap, plaster, chalk, wood, constructing with card, wood, wire, metal, plastics, found materials and kits;
- *work centred around play and drama* including puppetry, creating environments, theatrical design, etc.

Some examples of three-dimensional work carried out in schools may be classed as sculpture, while others relate more clearly to the design and technology curriculum. Many of the processes of construction are shared between the two subjects; both subjects can use the same materials, techniques and processes but to different ends. Very broadly, design and technology involves the conscious use of the design and problem solving processes to develop systems and artefacts which meet identified needs, while art and design is perhaps more orientated to the intuitive, personal and individual modes of thinking, expression, communication and construction of meaning.

Another way of thinking about sculpture is to identify the four fundamental processes it encompasses:

Box 3.9 Sculpture processes

Modelling – shaping 'plastic' materials: clay, Plasticine, salt dough.

Carving – starting with a block and removing material to reveal a form: stone, wood, or, in school, soap, wax, leather-hard clay, plaster blocks.

Construction – joining loose parts to create a form: building materials, wood, metal, mixed media, or, in school, 'junk modelling'- working with recycled packaging, cardboard, wood, etc.

Casting – creating a mould, usually from clay, and pouring in a self-hardening liquid medium, such as plaster.

Why work with sculpture?

In the early years, children experience and learn about the three-dimensional world and the space, objects and structures within it, through direct activity in movement and play. Provision of malleable materials, such as clay, Plasticine and dough, construction materials such as building blocks, together with water and sand provide not only a tactile experience and materials for investigation, but also media for representation, the three-dimensional equivalent of drawing and painting. Simple construction materials – cardboard boxes and tubes (recycled 'junk') – and joining devices (clips, pegs, rubber bands, sellotape and glue) give an opportunity to make a lasting artefact rather than something ephemeral which can be dismantled as with construction kits.

Children need to experience a wide variety of materials to understand the world they live in and clay, for example, is a fundamental, plastic, three-dimensional medium. Evidence of clay and ceramics is everywhere; much of the built environment is fashioned from ceramic bricks and tiles and domestic spaces such as kitchens and bathrooms invariably feature fired clay. Clay is perhaps one of the most ancient media for artistic expression in human history occurring naturally in the earth in many parts of the world. Figures, animals and simple, decorated containers have been found in most ancient cultures where clay was available in the local environment.

The most essential experience that clay provides is modelling soft clay. This provides a three-dimensional medium to realize impulses, feelings and ideas and construct meaningful artefacts. It is possible to provide this experience with just a bag of clay and, perhaps, some wooden tools. This is a good starting point and the lack of resources to fire and glaze clay should not be used as a reason to avoid clay, although, with more resources and understanding, a wider range of approaches and projects is possible.

Processes, strategies and practical considerations

Modelling

Modelling can be explored through dough, Plasticine and, particularly, through clay. Working with clay can be a hugely enriching and enjoyable experience for children throughout the 3–11 age range, and the potential of the process is explored in depth below.

- *Dough* can be baked or left to harden and painted. One recipe (salt dough) is to mix and knead equal quantities (300 g) of flour and salt with a tablespoon full of cooking oil and a small amount of water. If put in an airtight bag or container – and particularly if stored in a refrigerator – it will last a long time. Foods dyes can be used to colour the dough, added during mixing. This is a valuable material used widely in the Foundation Stage.
- *Plasticine* is also a useful, reusable, modelling material. When new, its coloured properties can be used expressively. However, unless colours are carefully separated, they will become intermixed. When cold, Plasticine can be difficult to mould, so it is best to warm it up before use. It is a useful, modelling material, particularly in the early years, but has quite different properties to clay and, as with dough, should not be seen as a substitute.

Casting

Papier mâché

Papier mâché (mashed paper) used to be made by soaking torn newspaper in water and mashing to form a stiff pulp. However, modern methods of paper-making mean it can now be very difficult to break newspaper down. Powdered paper can be ordered through suppliers' catalogues but kitchen rolls, or cheap toilet paper, can be used as a substitute. Cold-water paste is added and the resulting material can be modelled into any sort of shape. Pastes with fungicide must be avoided, as they are toxic and unsuitable for use with young children. PVA glue can also be added for extra strength.

A more versatile method is 'paper lamination' (also usually called papier mâché though not strictly correct). This is familiar to many from the practice of, for example, covering balloons with patches of glued newspaper. Torn strips of newspaper are painted with paste and laminated over a structure made from crumpled newspaper, balloons, recycled packaging, clay, Plasticine, card, wire, withies, wood, or a combination of these. Alternatively, strips and patches of newspaper can be laid into or over moulds, using cling film as a releasing agent or water only for the first layer, rather than glue, to avoid adhesion. These moulds could be containers or objects, or specially made from clay or Plasticine, for instance, in mask making. When dry, models can be painted and could be further strengthened by varnishing with matt, silk or glossy polyurethane varnish depending on the surface quality required. Papier mâché therefore ranges from 'plastic' modelling to mixed media construction and it has much potential as a cheap, yet versatile, three-dimensional medium in school encouraging problem-solving, designing, creativity and practical making skills.

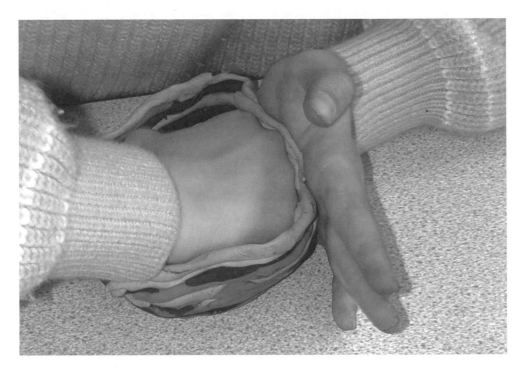

Figure 3.7 Using Plasticine in the early years

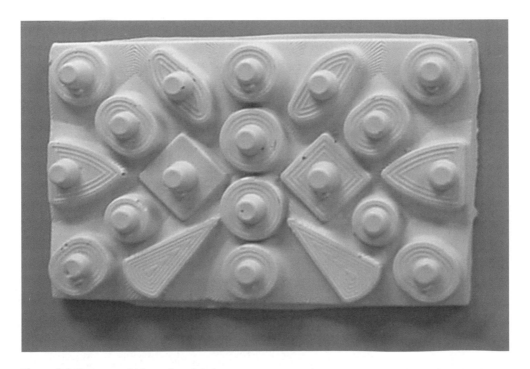

Figure 3.8 Plaster mould from chocolate box

Plaster of Paris and Mod-Roc

Plaster of Paris is a white powder, which is added to water, mixed and can then be poured into moulds. Moulds can easily be made from materials such as clay or Plasticine, for example. The plaster sets quite quickly, growing quite hot in the process. Once set, it can be carved or filed to refine shape and surface. Anyone who has broken a limb will be familiar with Plaster of Paris-impregnated bandages used to make casts to support the limb while the bones heal. This plaster bandage can be purchased from suppliers (one name is Mod-Roc). The bandages are dipped into water and can then be moulded onto a support, while they are still soft, to create sculptures. It is messy (so protective clothing must be worn) but exciting, and full of potential as a rapid sculptural construction material.

Working with clay

Clay can be worked in a variety of ways including modelling, carving, construction and casting and is consequently a versatile medium for a vast range of three-dimensional work.

Modelling with clay

Many testify to the unique feel and qualities of clay as a plastic, malleable material. The clay used in the classroom is a cleaned version of the clay found in the ground. Clay changes its properties according to the amount of water it contains, and is best worked with when it is soft and malleable but not sticky. In this state it can be joined, retain marks and impressions and, if not modelled too thinly, has a certain amount of structural strength. Children can be put off clay easily if it is not provided in the correct soft consistency for modelling. A good way of testing the consistency of clay is to hold a small ball in the hand and shape it just using finger pressure. If it is soft to model and holds its shape easily it is just right. It should not be sticky (too moist) or crack easily (too dry).

Clay shrinks as it dries and some clays have added ground fired clay – 'grog' – which helps to minimize shrinkage and stabilize the clay. Grogged clay feels rougher when hand building and it is a matter of preference whether grogged or plain clay is chosen.

Clays gain their colours from minerals that occur naturally: for instance red or terracotta clay contains iron oxide. The ideal clay for school is one that is light coloured when fired, enabling it to take coloured slips, glazes, paints, etc. It is also less likely to stain clothing. Such clay is Buff School Earthenware/Stoneware Clay available from most educational suppliers in 10 or 12 kg bags. It is smooth and grey coloured when wet. It dries to a light grey and when fired turns a light buff or off-white which takes paint or glaze colour very well. It is cheap enough not to have to worry about recycling dried clay.

When dry, clay is rigid but easily broken. It has to be thoroughly dry to be fired (baked to a high temperature) in a kiln, where it changes, becoming progressively harder and durable. This first firing is called 'biscuit firing'. Air-hardening clay ('Newclay') is available if, as is the case in many primary schools, there is no access to a kiln. However, this is more expensive; it is also full of fibres and so is, essentially, a different medium to real clay.

Carving, construction and casting with clay

As clay dries it becomes 'leather hard': more rigid and stronger, but less easy to bend and mould. In this state it can be carved or, if previously rolled into slabs or tiles, cut with a blunt knife and hand-built into geometric structures as a construction. In its 'sticky' or liquid state (slip) it can be used to join soft and leather-hard clay together as a kind of 'clay glue'. If care is taken to score or cross-hatch the surfaces to be joined before painting with slip a very good join is made which is as strong as the clay itself.

Pressing clay into a textured surface or pressing shapes into clay provides a surface which can be cast. Plaster of Paris can be mixed and poured into a clay mould.

Colouring and glazing clay

Clay can also be coloured and given a variety of surface treatments. Biscuit fired clay can be painted with ordinary classroom paints: blocks, powder or ready-mixed. Wetting the fired clay before it is painted is advisable as the biscuit fired clay is very porous. The painted object can then be varnished with matt, silk or glossy polyurethane varnish, depending on the surface quality required – although if this is to be done by the children it must be done with careful supervision, as these varnishes are not water based. Brushes should be cleaned by adults only, as white spirit is required.

If a kiln is available then children can have the real experience of glazed pottery. To colour and glaze clay work, it is a good idea, especially for non-specialists, to use 'under-glaze' colours (obtainable from suppliers of pottery materials and applied like powder paint) and one transparent glaze. This gives a whole range of colour that can be painted onto the leather hard clay immediately, and then biscuit-fired, or applied to biscuit fired work. The work is then dipped into the clear glaze and fired a second time (the glaze, or 'glost', firing). Only one glaze needs to be purchased, mixed and maintained. This system can be used successfully at all levels, from the early years and throughout the primary years.

Organization for working with clay

All that is needed to begin clay work is a bag of clay, some sponges and perhaps some shaped lollipop sticks to use as clay tools.

- Health and safety: clay is a safe, clean material – kaolin clay is used in medicines to settle the stomach! It is only dangerous as dry dust – an irritant when breathed in. Like any dust, if inhaled over a long period of time, it can lead to respiratory problems. For this reason, cleaning up is important and should be with a 'wet regime' using sponges and mops rather than scraping and brushing.
- The pupils will need aprons or protective clothing of some sort.
- Pupils need to be able work on a surface that can be easily sponged down. Formica tables are excellent. Some teachers like to cover tables with plasticized cloth for clay work but clay worked directly on to a shiny surface will stick – therefore it should either be held in the hand or done on a small, wooden board or old, sugar/brushwork paper. Wooden

boards are slightly absorbent so the clay will release easily and they can also be used to transport delicate work to a shelf while it dries. Thin, exterior-quality plywood is ideal.

- It is best to work over an easily cleaned floor, which can be mopped if necessary. If children are trained to remain at their tables while working and to pick up any clay which falls on the floor, it is surprising how little mess is created. Clay droppings can be swept up while still damp but not when dry. Dry clay bits when trodden on become dust that is easily transferred elsewhere as footprints, and into the air as dust. Putting a plastic sheet on the floor is not advised as it can be tripped over or slid on. Boards and tools should have lumps of clay removed before being sponged clean in the sink.

- Many of the problems faced by teachers working with clay are caused by pupils having access to water. Clay begins to dry from the moment it is removed from the bag or clay bin and this process speeds up as the clay becomes warm from the hands. The best practice is to supply each pupil or pair of pupils with a damp sponge in a plastic tray, which they can use from time to time to keep their hands moist and then for keeping the clay at a working consistency. Some teachers even go so far as to put a board over the sink while work is going on! It is a natural thing for a pupil to want to wet the clay but once this has happened the whole lump becomes a slimy mess and there is no alternative but to start again.

- Storing clay: plastic clay is delivered ready for use in strong airtight plastic bags sealed with a wire twist. Providing the bag has not been punctured it will keep in this state for months, even years. The consistency can be felt by squeezing the clay through the bag. Children can be given the clay directly from the bag, which should be kept closed when not in use. Even leaving it open for half an hour can affect the consistency. Bags that have begun to dry out in this way can be reconstituted by spraying or splashing water down the insides of the bag around the clay and then resealing. The clay evenly absorbs the water over a day or two. This can be repeated until the right consistency is achieved. Bags that have been punctured should be sealed in another bag, used immediately or transferred to the clay bin.

- The clay bin: classrooms should have a clay bin where recycled clay can be stored in small lumps ready for use. The best clay bins are medium-sized, plastic dustbins with lids which can be sealed airtight. The clay is best stored in fist size lumps so that the damp air can circulate to the bottom of the bin. The clay is covered with a damp cloth – an old towel or double layer of Hessian – then a piece of polythene, or an opened-out clay bag, is laid on top of the damp cloth and finally sealed in by the bin lid. The cloth needs to be kept damp so that the clay will be in the right soft condition to use. At the end of a working session all the unused clay should be reconstituted – by kneading (wedging) to get rid of air bubbles and gain a smooth consistency – and put back in the bin for reuse. The lid should always be put back on the bin when not in use, even during a session. Pupils should learn about this method as part of the process of working with clay so that they can help maintain the system. Unused dry clay can be reconstituted by soaking down in bins, drying to the non-sticky, plastic state on a wooden board and then wedging it. (Children can learn how to do this to prepare the clay for use.) However, for most teachers it will be more cost effective to throw away dried clay and replace it with new clay, as the reconstituting process takes too much time, effort, equipment and space.

Practical activities with clay

If pupils have not worked with clay for some time, it is a good idea to give them a chance to explore the material by giving them some quick exercises that encourage them to discover the full range of expressive and structural possibilities before moving on to project work. This also develops 'clever hands', good hand-eye-brain coordination, and builds an instinctual appreciation of the nature of the medium. It is often beneficial to teach skills as these enable children to be more creative. Below is just a selection of possible activities to allow children to explore the qualities and possibilities of clay and learn skills.

- Holes: start by modelling a spherical shape, gently push holes into it (one hand is needed to support the sphere), model-stretch-support-move, until a hollow ball full of holes is created.
- Projections: starting with a spherical shape, using straight fingers to gradually pull up conical shapes (this is a very strong shape), smooth over cracks at all times, try to use all the fingers when pulling and keep the pressure even.
- Coils: practise hand rolling coils, try to keep the pressure even to obtain an even coil. Practise making a coil pot with a circular or square base smoothing the coils so that they are worked together on at least one side (inner or outer) using fingers or a wooden tool.
- Thumb pots: supporting a ball of clay in a cupped hand, gradually press out a hole with the thumb of the other hand, rotating the ball. Smooth out the pot, until it is no thinner than one centimetre and is semi-spherical in shape. Flatten the rim by gently tapping it on the table.
- Spheres: make two identical thumb pots. Join the rims by roughening, cross-hatching (scoring) the surfaces. Paint on some slip (liquid clay) and gently push together, supporting with the hands and gradually smoothing the join. Make a small hole in the hollow sphere before leaving to dry to allow quicker drying (and prevent explosions if firing!). This basic shape can be used to model fruit and natural form, or the bodies of animals, portrait heads, etc.
- Rolling out clay: sugar paper or a wooden board is needed to prevent the clay from sticking to the table (hessian, which is often used by potters, can collect too much dust). Use two batons that should be the same as the depth required for the clay (1 cm is a good thickness). The clay is roughly shaped towards the size and shape of the final slab and placed between the batons. Roll the clay out using a rolling pin, lifting the clay up from time to time, to allow it to expand.
- Formers: use existing forms such as cardboard tubes and blocks of wood, to support the clay while it dries. Wrap newspaper around the former first (to stop the clay sticking). Roll out slabs of clay and wrap around the former, joining together using the cross-hatching and slip method. When leather hard, extract the former and newspaper before the clay shrinks and becomes dry and brittle.
- Carving: when the clay is leather hard, it may be carved, or projections and additions can be joined using the cross-hatching and slip method.

Alongside learning skills, children should always be encouraged to explore the creative possibilities of clay or to engage in project work. Children will have their own ideas about what they want to make; other work might be a response to stimuli provided by the teacher or an aspect of an ongoing project:

- People: start with a ball of clay and pull out projections for the arms, legs and head. All the fingers can be used in modelling, keeping the pressure even. 'Clothes' can be made using thin, hand-made slabs of clay wrapped and smoothed onto the figure. 'Hair' can be made by pushing clay through a sieve and joining to the head with slip. Challenging children to make smaller versions of their figures will be a test of their fine motor skills.
- Slabs can be used to make tiles, model furniture, houses, or used as surfaces to impress or build with texture.
- Unusual creatures can be constructed by adding to a basic sphere.
- Observations of natural artefacts and how they are constructed (for example, shells, seed pods, plants) can encourage children to experiment with form.

Textiles

Textiles provide an exciting range of possibilities for work with children in the Foundation Stage and primary age phase. The resources that are used, from different types and textures of fabrics and threads, to colourful dyes, engage children's imagination and interest. The outcomes are not always predictable and the unexpected results of processes such as batik and tie-dye can very often be visually rich, bringing a rewarding sense of achievement and confidence. At the same time, there are processes and skills to be learned and developed that will enable children to gain more control of the media and help them to realize their own ideas and improve their work.

When working with textiles it may be tempting for teachers to be overprescriptive about the end product. The 'here's one I made earlier' approach, where children are expected to reproduce a given example, is not good practice, and should be avoided except, perhaps, in the very specific context of demonstrating a particular practical technique. If activities do not extend beyond this they do not amount to art and design *education*. It is important to see textiles as another, important range of media and processes through which children can explore and develop their own ideas, and as an important means of introducing children to the concept of surface design and decoration.

Why work with textiles?

Textiles are often underrated as media in art and design. This should be addressed from the outset. Sometimes, work with textiles is described as 'craft' rather than art. Often, student teachers consider themselves to have no artistic abilities at all, not taking into account that they have worked creatively in designing and making clothing or decorative artefacts for the home, using fabric, thread and dyes in one form or another. They have not seen their work as a form of 'art and design', and in this they are probably reflecting the way that working with textiles has predominantly been viewed within Western art traditions. One explanation for the apparent lack of recognition of such work might be that it is traditionally often carried out by women. It is well known that, historically, women's art work has been marginalized by the mainstream art world in Western Europe (see Chapter 8). In many cultural contexts textiles are a dominant and particularly rich form of art and design, whereas the emphasis in post-Renaissance, Western European contexts has tended to be on the 'fine arts' of painting, drawing and sculpture. If we are going to present children with a more inclusive view of art and design, then work with textiles should be seen as offering an equally valid and meaningful range of processes and media.

Almost any idea or response can be represented through fabric as readily as any other medium. If children are encouraged to acquire understanding and skill in the full range of media, including textiles, then they can decide when and whether textiles suit their purposes. This can be to record their observations as well as to work imaginatively. (See practical activity examples at the end of this section.)

Work with textiles clearly lends itself to an exploration of the visual element of texture. The surface quality of different fabrics and threads and yarns and the textures that can be created by collage and appliqué can provide tactile experiences not necessarily available in other media. This is particularly rewarding for children who have visual impairment. Textiles also provide children with plenty of opportunities for thinking about colour, shape and pattern.

Processes, strategies and practical considerations

There are a number of different processes for working with textiles. Most of these have traditionally been used and developed in different societies over a long period, and can be adapted for use in the primary classroom. Some involve specific techniques for applying colour and pattern to fabric (batik, tie-dye); others entail layering of fabric (collage or appliqué, 'reverse' appliqué); others require the use of stitches (embroidery) and the addition of decoration such as beads. There is also the construction of fabric through, for example, weaving, knitting, felt making and patchwork.

Batik

This is very popular with children and adults alike! It is a 'resist' method, which, in general terms, involves the application of a waterproof material to a surface, which will resist any water based medium, such as paint or dye, that is then applied. Batik is a technique that is widespread in Indonesia and Malaysia and also China and other parts of South East, South and Central Asia. Hot wax is applied to fabric; as it penetrates the fabric and cools, it resists any dye that is applied. The dye will obviously need to be the cold-water sort, as hot dye would melt the wax. Dylon, or non-toxic, specialist batik dyes provided by educational suppliers can be used. (Generally, for all processes involving cold-water dyes, the work will need to be 'fixed' by applying 'dye-fix' that can be purchased for this purpose, to make the colour fast and therefore washable. This is only a concern, however, if the work will need to be washed at any point.) After being immersed in one colour, the work can be allowed to dry and then more wax added and the fabric dyed with a different colour. In this way a design of different colours can be built up. At the end of the process, the wax is removed. The process requires the child to think through their design logically, working out how to apply the wax and what the colours will be and bearing in mind that wherever the wax is applied, it will protect the colour underneath it. There is a need to work from lighter to darker colours as each colour is laid over the previous one: a light yellow will have little effect on a dark blue, whereas a blue applied to yellow will create green. For successful batik the children will need to be provided with fine, cotton fabric (e.g. cotton lawn), rather than synthetic material. To help the wax penetrate it is best for the fabric to be stretched across an open wooden, rectangular frame (adjustable ones can be obtained from suppliers), but, if these are not available, the wax can usually be applied successfully by laying the fabric (ensuring it is flat and ironing it if necessary) on a piece of clean sugar paper.

The tools required are a batik stove or wax pot (there are some relatively inexpensive plastic stoves, with a metal liner; alternatively there are more expensive, all metal versions). Bags of wax 'beads' specifically for the purpose can be obtained from suppliers and are melted in the stove. *Tjantings* are traditional tools that consist of a wooden handle attached to a small brass or copper 'bowl' with a short pipe or tube at the end as an outlet (different sizes allow for different thickness of mark). These are used to scoop up the hot wax which flows onto the fabric through the outlet. Children will need to learn how to control the *tjanting* so they can draw with it and will need to be shown that the wax must be sufficiently hot to flow freely onto the fabric and penetrate it. If it isn't hot enough, the wax will sit on the surface of the fabric rather than permeating it, and dye will seep underneath it. If this begins to happen the *tjanting* needs to be returned to the wax pot to warm up, and to collect some hotter wax. Sometimes the wax can be too hot and will flow out too quickly. With experience children will learn how to control the process, but early experimental efforts will still achieve results. Clearly, children need appropriate adult supervision during their activity to ensure that they use the hot wax safely.

At the end of the process the fabric can be left to dry and then the wax can be removed with a hot iron. Layers of newspaper underneath and on top of the fabric will soak up the wax as it melts, and can be discarded as they become saturated. A piece of plain newsprint or kitchen paper should be used next to the fabric, to prevent ink from transferring from newspaper to fabric.

An alternative and quicker method is to apply the whole of the design at once and then to paint on the coloured dyes. To understand the principles of wax resist, without using hot wax, children can use candles on paper and brush over with watercolour, but with appropriate supervision even young children can be given the opportunity to work with melted wax on fabric. If a teacher decides this is unsuitable, a form of batik with younger children, especially in the Foundation Stage, can be achieved using cold-water paste of some sort (e.g. flour and water paste), which can be put on to the fabric instead

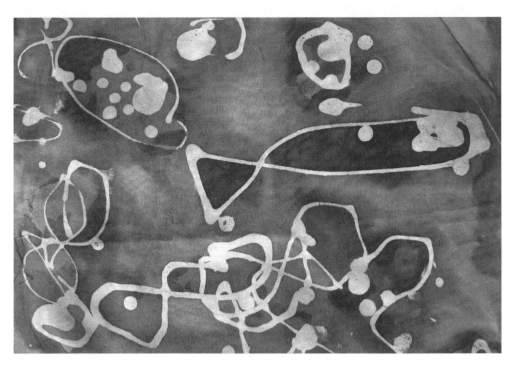

Figure 3.9 Experimenting with batik

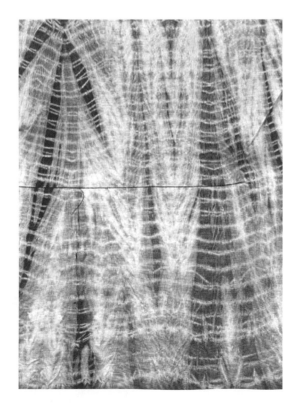

Figure 3.10 Experimenting with tie-dye

of the hot wax. A gelled, water-based ink such as screen-printing ink or acrylic paint can then be applied (remembering that acrylic paint is difficult to remove from clothing).

Tie-dye

This is another form of 'resist', where the fabric is tied with twine or string to restrict the flow of dye through the fabric, thereby creating a pattern. Again it is widespread as a means of applying pattern to fabric and can be found in Asia and Africa, for example. It is a relatively straightforward process. Children can be encouraged to experiment with tying fabric in different ways, pleating or knotting or tying beads, beans or pebbles into it. A difficulty which younger children may have is in tying tightly enough. It is important to remember to immerse the tied fabric in water and let it soak, before putting it into the dye. This allows the fibres to swell, making the knots tighter. The fabric can be tied further and immersed in different colours of dye – again working from lighter to darker colours, to create more complex and colourful patterns. As with all textile work involving dyes, natural fabrics should be used as they usually take dye better than synthetic fabrics. As well as creating pieces of patterned fabric other fabric items can be designed and dyed, such as imaginative flags, banners, bags or cotton tents, and children will also enjoy dyeing clothing such as t-shirts. Most educational suppliers will have a range of dyes that are suitable for tie-dye.

Collage and appliqué

The basic process of collage and appliqué is to cut out shapes from fabric and stitch them onto a base piece of fabric in order to build up designs and pictures. Sometimes intricate patterns are cut out, or more than one layer of fabric is applied. A technique sometimes called reverse appliqué, and used in the 'mola' work of Central America, involves having two layers of fabric (say, two rectangles, one on top of the other) and then cutting out shapes in the top layer, to reveal the fabric beneath. Some pieces of work combine the two methods.

Many examples of appliqué can be found around the world – for example, in Guatemala, Panama, India, China and Egypt. Typically, the cut edges of the fabric are carefully turned under and stitched. Children can be encouraged to stitch, but they can also stick the fabric on – this can be particularly useful when the child is focusing on creating a design or picture, as the stitching can be very time-consuming. Children will enjoy adding creative stitching to their work as well as beads, sequins and buttons.

A good example of the way in which fabric collage has been used can be found in the picture books by Jeannie Baker, who photographs her collages (for example, Baker, J. 1991). Children may be familiar with her books as they are often in school libraries.

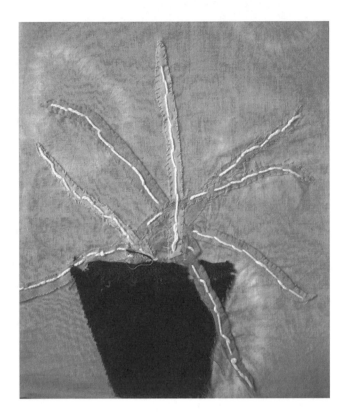

Figure 3.11 Fabric collage (appliqué)

Embroidery

Again, there are rich traditions of embroidery in almost all parts of the world, from 'black work' in the north of England to the embroidered belts and purses of China. Children can be taught traditional embroidery stitches, such as running stitch, back stitch, cross stitch, chain stitch, satin stitch and French knots, and these can be combined in many different ways. Embroidery offers much more, however, than working with traditional stitching. By focusing on design, colour and texture children can create rich pieces of work, selecting the threads and yarns they need to realize their ideas and using stitching imaginatively and creatively, perhaps breaking some of the 'rules'. Embroidery can be combined with other processes, such as tie-dye and collage. Beads, buttons, sequins and other materials such as feathers, felt, wool, etc. can be incorporated imaginatively into the work. Children should be encouraged to develop their own ideas and explore the possibilities of the materials.

Printing

All of the ways of making prints discussed in the printmaking section of this chapter can be applied to fabric. A smooth, finely woven fabric will provide a clear print, and it is best if the fabric is stretched onto a smooth surface and secured with tape, before printing. For best results, a thin sheet of foam, covered with a sheet of plastic, can be fixed to a table to make a more or less permanent fabric printing surface. The fabric to be printed can be stretched across this. The same water based inks that are used on paper will print on fabric, but there are specialist fabric printing inks available as well. Again, water-based inks should be used with children, but the printed fabric will not be washable unless the ink is fixed.

Constructing fabric: weaving; felt making; knitting; patchwork

Weaving

Weaving is a widespread art form and while the basic process is common to all cultures, there are variations, such as the *ikat* of Indonesia, where threads are tie-dyed before being woven. Traditional, simple weaving can be achieved using card looms or rectangular wooden frames so that yarn can be wound round to create the warp threads. The under and over process of weaving is a familiar one and can be done using the fingers, a large blunt needle or a 'shuttle' made out of card. Children can tend to pull the yarn too tightly so that the piece of weaving narrows in the middle. To avoid this they can cut off each thread when they have taken it across, leaving sufficient at the end to tie it off.

Again, children should be encouraged to explore the possibilities of the tools and materials – for example, looms can be constructed in different shapes and sizes; tree branches and twigs, bound together, can be used to create unusual forms. Weaving provides a good opportunity to explore texture and children can be encouraged to experiment with weaving materials other than yarn. Strips of paper, fabric, even plastic bags, and all sorts of other 'found' materials can be woven in.

Felt making

Felt making uses raw fleece that is washed and dyed. The basic process is to dampen and rub the wool until the fibres are matted together. This can be achieved by spreading out several layers of fleece (different colours of the fleece can be arranged to form a design) between two pieces of cotton fabric (on top of a sheet of plastic or in the bottom of a bowl). Each layer should be pulled out so that the fibres are in line and the next layer placed at right angles to the previous one, and as each layer is added, the fleece should be soaked in a solution of soapy water, using soap flakes and hot water. The second piece of cotton fabric is laid on top, saturated again so that the surface is slippery, and the whole is pressed down and rubbed all over with the palms of the hands, until the fleece fibres are stuck together. This can take some time, and the fleece will shrink to form a smaller piece of felt.

Knitting

Knitting might not immediately come to mind, but it offers another means of constructing textiles. Once the basic techniques are mastered, there are many creative possibilities for designing patterns, using shape and colour and textured wools and yarn. The same applies to other processes, such as crochet.

Patchwork

There are rich traditions of patchwork, in almost all cultures, and fine examples are American quilts. Patchwork involves the tessellation of shapes cut from fabric to create a larger piece of fabric, often using scraps or old clothing. Templates for the design can be cut from thin card. Pieces of fabric are cut to the appropriate shape and size, leaving sufficient to tuck under, and are then pinned and tacked (preliminary stitching that can be easily removed) to the card so that the fabric covers the edges. The pieces are then joined together with tiny stitches to form the larger piece. Children can investigate traditional designs or experimental possibilities and the process is perhaps best carried out collaboratively so that a larger piece can be created in less time.

Organization for textiles

For children to gain the widest understanding of the possibilities of working with textiles they will need to be provided with an imaginative range of resources as well as appropriate tools.

Key considerations:

- Variety is the key for fabrics, threads and yarns. They should be selected and collected in abundance and for their different colours and textures. All sorts of scraps can be used: wools; ribbons; tape; string; beads; off-cuts of fabric – the list is endless.
- Resources need to be readily available for the children and sorted so that they can be easily accessed. Suitable base fabrics should be kept in good condition.
- A clean iron should be available for smoothing fabrics before use and another iron for removing wax for batik.
- Remember that scissors that are allowed to be used for cutting paper will not easily cut fabric and, if necessary, for safety reasons, sharp fabric scissors can be kept aside by the teacher, to be used under proper supervision.
- A range of different sized-needles will be essential for embroidery.
- Buckets or bowls will be needed for dyes.

Although the processes have been described individually, children can be encouraged to explore ways of combining different processes in their work. For example,

- A piece of tie-dyed fabric can be used as a base for a collage and embroidery can then be added.
- There are different kinds of fabric paints and crayons (available from suppliers) and while these can be used on their own, they can also be used to add further marks to a piece of work, or on fabric that is later cut up to be used in collage.

Teachers might endeavour to collect examples of textiles created in different ways and in different cultural contexts, which can be used as inspiration as well as to demonstrate the results that different processes achieve.

- There are many examples in shops that sell fabrics by the metre as well as in clothing and items for the home such as cushions and bedcovers.
- It can be interesting for children to work out how different results have been achieved. If pieces can be acquired from people who have collected examples from countries in the south, there may be clues as to how they were made, such as the stiffness or smell of wax in pieces of batik from Indonesia or needle holes or bits of thread remaining in stitched ('controlled') tie-dye from India or China. Many traditionally made textiles will have been created using natural dyes, such as indigo.

Working with textiles provides exciting opportunities for cross-curricular learning. For example:

- if learning how to make dyes from natural materials, such as berries and nettles, children can carry out scientific investigations;
- patchwork includes mathematical thinking around tessellation;
- learning about different traditions in working with textiles can entail historical and geographical enquiry;
- investigating basic processes such as preparing and spinning wool from raw fleece ready for weaving will help children develop scientific and technological concepts.

Practical activity examples

- A Year 4 child was making a book about his experiments with growing seeds. He decided that he wanted to cover his book with fabric and to create a fabric collage representing the growth of a bean, so he went to great lengths to dye pieces of white felt, experimenting with different shades of green to achieve his desired result. He was fascinated by the gradual change on the bean's shoot from white to green and liked the way that the dye, seeping through the felt, could capture this.
- Children (Year 2) who were being introduced to using hot wax on fabric, for batik, had been closely observing mini-beasts and were keen to record their observations of the creatures using a *tjanting* as a drawing tool. On other occasions, they appreciated the imaginative possibilities of working in batik, or fabric collage, to interpret their visit to the pond in the park, or to experiment with colour, texture and shape.
- Children in Year 5 had tied fabric in different ways, for instance, by pleating it in long, narrow folds and tying these in a bundle (creating a 'concertina' pattern) or by tying large knots in the centre of the fabric to create a 'sunburst' pattern. While there was some control over the outcome, the results could not be known until the piece was untied. As with printmaking, the children could extend their visual vocabulary through evaluating unintended marks and features. They could also explore unintended meanings in what they had produced.

Collage

Collage is a process that can be perfectly simple or endlessly complex: it is an area of the art and design curriculum that is accessible to all. Essentially, a collage is a flat image or design that is constructed from a selection of materials. A collage might be constructed from paper, card or fabric; it might juxtapose photographic images, or it might be assembled on a computer screen from images that have been scanned and manipulated. Approaches to making contemporary collage can be traced back to the Cubists working a century ago, when Picasso and Braque incorporated newspapers and other objects into their paintings, an approach Picasso was later to explore in his sculptures.

Why make collages?

Advantages

Collage appeals to children because it is essentially about transformation: torn strips of paper could become an autumn landscape, while Frankenstein's monster might emerge from the contents of a rubbish bin. Many children are discouraged from making art because they believe that being able to draw accurately is a prerequisite for creativity. Collage activities offer valuable opportunities for children to experiment with colour, composition and texture without needing to make realistically representational images. Children can experiment with compositions by arranging materials before fixing them – the constant call for the rubber need not be heard. The wide range and accessibility of collage materials encourages children to appreciate the egalitarian nature of art, and demonstrates that they need not visit the art shop to invest in a range of resources.

Artists who make collages often reveal their awareness of the potential of the medium for helping us to see something new in the familiar. A collage may be exciting because of the way it juxtaposes one image against another in an interesting or unexpected way –artists often use this to humorous, dramatic or poignant effect. Teachers will find that collage activities offer opportunities to expand on a recycling theme raised in Science or Geography lessons; they will also appreciate that a collage lesson is cheap and easy to resource, as materials are often free – using them to make art is a little like making a meal from scraps in the fridge.

Challenges

While children will enjoy the freedom offered by collage, a feeling that 'anything goes' can be problematic. Collage activities can sometimes become chaotic and muddled, and will need some planning and structure to ensure that the work is meaningful for children. Large-scale pieces can be extremely effective – but the process of constructing them can sometimes become boring and repetitive – individuals might prefer to work on a small scale, while large-scale projects could be more happily attempted by groups.

Mosaics often inspire many of the collages made in primary and nursery schools, and the resulting pieces often lack ambition. Teachers should discourage children from

Figure 3.12 Collage at the Foundation Stage, inspired by Kandinsky

cutting large quantities of small squares from a few sheets of coloured paper and assembling them into collages – the finished pieces will lack depth and variety. Equally lacking in value is the task of screwing up and sticking down little balls of tissue paper to make an image, which children are sometimes asked to do. This does little to advance children's understanding or skill in art and design: it is no more educationally worthwhile than 'colouring in'. Photographs cut from magazines offer a richer range of colours and tones, and these fragments can quickly be assembled into 'palettes' of colour that will form the basis of more interesting collages. The properties and potential of tissue paper can be explored more thoroughly through activities that encourage children to layer the paper in a way that enables them to explore multiple tones and combinations of colours.

Children should also be given practice in handling and applying glue. Applying too small an amount will result in their masterpieces falling in fragments all over the floor; applying too much can result in works of art that sit in soggy heaps for the rest of the term. Encouraging children to work with small quantities of glue will mean that there is less chance of children cementing themselves to their desks. They can also experiment with thinning PVA glue with water to create a thin varnish that can be applied over the top of a collage to seal in the contents.

Figure 3.13 Mixed-media collage at the Foundation Stage: self portrait

Organization for collage

1 Magazines are a great source of colour and images for collage: their availability and strong colours mean that they are ideal for use in large-scale group work.

2 Encourage children to begin by amassing palettes of colour from magazines, scrap paper or other sources. This is an opportunity to draw children's attention to the wide range of tones to be found within one colour – a single magazine can produce an almost endless variety.

3 Tearing rough shapes from paper will give the children's work an energetic quality – however, many children lack experience of using scissors efficiently, and collage is a good opportunity for them to practise this skill.

4 When applying cut or torn pieces, children should spread glue thinly over large areas before placing several pieces down – switching frequently from spreading to sticking can become tedious.

5 Sometimes the wide range of colours available to children can bewilder them. Encourage them to experiment with restricted palettes, e.g. blues, greens, purples.

6 Collages need not be fixed and permanent – objects might be arranged into a composition, photographed and dismantled for reuse.

7 In the early years, children respond positively to the tactile qualities of resources chosen for collage. Feel free to get the lentils out, but ensure that children have access to a range of materials such as tissue paper, string, etc.

8 Collages can be made using textiles, where fabric is stuck onto a base fabric (or stiff paper) or stitched down (appliqué). Remember that children will become frustrated if they are using scissors that do not cut fabric effectively (usually scissors that have been used regularly for cutting paper will be too blunt). Further information on fabric collage will be found in the 'Textiles' section of this chapter.

9 Children with visual impairments may respond positively to being provided with a range of textures that can be combined into tactile compositions.

10 Introduce children to a range of work by artists who have used collage; locating images via a search engine is an effective way of doing this.

11 When planning collage activities, help the children to decide what the focus should be – the materials or the image. Are they interested in exploring a range of materials and experimenting with unusual combinations? Or is the intention to create a recognizable image from the materials gathered?

12 Make use of materials found in the recycling centre that can be used for art and design projects.

13 Having too specific an idea in mind from the beginning of the work can often hamper the development of a piece. Encourage children to let the process of making a collage influence its direction – accidents will happen, but often they turn out for the best!

Practical activities

1 Making collages inspired by paintings is an excellent way to draw children's attention to the detail of a composition, as well as providing valuable opportunities for children to engage in group work. Take a reproduction of a painting and divide it into a number of sections of equal size. Picasso's 'Guernica' is a good example of a painting to choose for this activity, as there is something happening in every corner of the composition. Children can work individually or in pairs on their section of the collage, before reassembling the sections to form the original composition. Teachers need to be clear about the learning opportunities in this activity so that it is not merely a reproduction of the painting for its own sake, or to make a nice display.

2 Encourage children to identify interesting details from a composition and use them as the basis for a composition of repeated patterns. Cutting shapes carefully from card should leave 'negative' shapes behind that can then be used in further compositions.

3 Younger children can explore silhouettes of objects – begin by making outline drawings of individual objects without worrying about detail, then use the outline as a guide within which materials can be collaged.

4 Magazines can be used as a source of images as well as colour – challenge children to select from magazines a handful of images that they think will provide interesting or amusing contrasts; cut carefully around the outline of each and integrate into a composition – remember that images can overlap.

5 Coloured tissue paper collages make effective 'stained glass' windows. Take a sheet of acetate (A4 transparent sleeves opened out to A3 are useful), spread a thin layer of PVA glue across it and make a composition of torn tissue paper – experiment with overlapping pieces to 'mix' tones and colours.

6 Make collage faces composed of features cut from magazines; this can link with experiments with mixing a range of flesh colours in paint.

7 Eric Carle's picture books, such as *The Very Hungry Caterpillar* (1969), are a useful resource as they feature a range of effective collages created from painted and torn paper strips. *Window* (1991), and other books by Jeannie Baker also feature some striking collages.

8 Place objects, shapes and textures onto a scanner – scan, rearrange, rescan, then collage different arrangements together in an image-editing programme such as Adobe Photoshop.

9 Further photographic collages can be made by inserting scanned figures onto a new background – try creating an imaginary sculpture garden by digitally pasting photographs of children's sculptures on to a background image.

ICT

ICT is an increasingly important part of the primary curriculum as a whole and of art and design in particular, and as a tool for learning and experimentation it sits comfortably alongside the more established practical processes covered in this chapter. Even at the Foundation Stage, very young children can explore software that provides them with opportunities to make virtual paintings, to experiment with a range of tools and techniques and to create a range of images and effects.

Older children, meanwhile, rapidly learn that computers offer ways of experimenting with composition, with colour, even with layers of images in ways that are just as direct and as valid as those carried out in other practical processes. Imagine, for example, a child pausing before adding a second or third colour to his/her print: the wrong decision at this point might threaten to undo hours of work. Using art and design software to experiment with potential colour combinations is a way of exploring potential solutions to a practical problem, all with a minimum of risk.

ICT processes, strategies and practical considerations

The ICT processes that are relevant to learning in art and design can generally be divided into:

1 those that enable children to create images from a 'blank canvas';
2 those that enable children to manipulate an existing image.

Technology changes at such a rapid rate that to recommend a list of software programs for use in the classroom would quickly become dated. Instead, it might be helpful to imagine two teachers, each finding him/herself placed in one of two extremes: one in an early years classroom with the bare minimum of ICT equipment, and the other working with older children and with the latest hi-tech resources.

The National Curriculum Online is a useful resource that aims to support teachers planning links between ICT and all core and foundation subjects. It helps pupils to learn in art and design by providing opportunities not only to develop their *creativity and imagination* but also to engage in *visual research* using the internet and other sources.

Creativity and imagination

Using ICT can help pupils to:

1 access, select and interpret information;
2 review and modify their work to improve the quality;
3 communicate with others and present information;
4 evaluate their work;
5 improve efficiency;
6 be creative and take risks;
7 gain confidence and independence.

Visual research

Using ICT can help pupils to:

1 gain greater autonomy in the selection of their materials;
2 take risks and explore ideas through saving multiple versions of their work;
3 experiment extensively when working with traditional media;
4 combine sound, image and movement, for example, in creating video and animation;
5 collaborate on developing art and design work with a wider range of people;
6 offer new tools and new ways to publish, present and communicate meaning, e.g. online galleries;
7 gain access to a wider range of artists, craftspeople and designers;
8 explore the nature and history of digital media.

(adapted from National Curriculum in Action www.ncaction.org.uk)

The Foundation Stage and Key Stage 1

Even the most ancient of computers should be able to run software programs that enable activities that begin with a 'blank canvas' (note how much of the terminology of digital imaging is borrowed from the traditions of art and design). The simplest 'paint' program – the type that comes packaged with most PCs – can be used effectively in the classroom, and may prove sufficient for children at the Foundation Stage and Key Stage 1. Such packages may only enable users to work on one document at a time – one will need to be saved and closed before opening or creating another – however, there are still opportunities to work across different versions of a document and for one child to extend the work made by another.

Most young children begin using art packages in two ways: first, they try to recreate the kinds of figurative drawings and paintings they happily make on paper (Mum, Dad, Dog, Me); second, they make a composition of random marks that tends to lack structure or individuality. While children may enjoy exploring both of these approaches, even a minimal amount of teacher intervention can rapidly move children forward, and even a limited set of tools can offer children opportunities to make interesting, challenging and engaging images.

As well as providing children with a choice of size and style of brush, and of a (limited) range of colours, basic packages should also offer facilities for selecting sections of an image, as well as for rotating, reflecting and 'flipping' selections. With a little support, the effects of these functions can quickly be explored by young children and the results can prompt them to reflect on the extent to which they are able to control the development of their images on the computer.

Box 3.10 Practical activity: repeating and rotating patterns

1 Begin by giving children freedom to use the paint program to explore the ways in which they can quickly create a range of colours and shapes.

2 Show children how to make a selection from the image they have created. They could use a rectangular 'marquee' to do this, or a looser 'lassoo'.

3 Use the menu (or keyboard shortcut) to copy this selection to the clipboard.

4 Open a new document and paste the selection in.

5 Repeat this several times and show children how to move the selections around to create a repeat pattern.

6 Some children will be able to extend this activity by 'flipping' and rotating the selection to create more complex patterns.

Key Stage 2

More sophisticated computer systems offer a wider range of ways in which children can experiment with digital imaging. Images that have been scanned in to the computer from a printed image, or loaded from a digital camera, can easily form the basis of experimental activities that not only require children to learn about the effects of a number of tools but also offer them opportunities to create individual and unique images.

Box 3.11 Practical activity: changing faces

The aim of this activity is to use art and design software to manipulate portraits. By following a sequence of steps, children will extend their knowledge of the functions of several tools and their awareness of the ways in which they can change the images they work on.

1 Begin by providing children with a digital camera with which they can take portraits of each other, then load the images onto the computer and open one up in a software package such as Adobe Photoshop.

2 Use the 'lasso' selection tool to trace around one of the eyes. Controlling the movement of the tool is tricky at first, but children need not be too accurate at this stage.

3 Once a loop around the eye has been completed, the dotted line will turn into a line of 'marching ants' – now 'Edit' and 'Copy' to copy this selection, then 'Edit' and 'Paste' to paste it in as a new layer. (Children should remember to save their work at each stage.)

> **4** Use the 'Move' tool to move the new eye to its new position; then in the Edit' menu, select 'Transform' and the 'Scale' option and adjust the scale by dragging on one of the corners (note – hold the 'shift' key down to retain the same proportions).
>
> **5** Do the same for the rest of the features – then experiment with colours. From the 'Image' menu, select 'Adjustments' and choose the 'Colour balance' option. You can then experiment with a range of alterations to the colours in the image.

More practical activities

Regular shapes, repeat patterns

Demonstrate to children how to use a drawing program to create an equilateral triangle, then copy and paste the triangle several times to make a repeat pattern. Experiment with arrangements of rows, blocks, etc. Then challenge children to 'paint' the triangles using as few colours as possible, but without making two adjacent triangles the same colour.

Distorting portraits

Many art and design software packages allow images to be easily manipulated. Scan children's drawings or load portraits from a digital camera and demonstrate how to use image manipulation software to stretch and distort their features into monstrous proportions.

Photographic sequences

Provide children with a digital camera and ask them to take 'action' photographs of their friends (a PE lesson would be ideal – for example, a sequence of pictures that demonstrates how to climb the climbing frame). Your computer should give you the option to print each of the photographs on a small scale. Print and cut around the photographs, paste the sequence around the edge of a frame and choose the best shot to enlarge for the centre. (Examples of Edward Muybridge's fascinating sequences of images depicting movement are easily located on the internet.)

Manipulating text

Children enjoy playing with the appearance of text onscreen; Lauren Child's books, such as *I Will Never Not Ever Eat a Tomato* feature wonderfully expressive use of typography that will inspire children's experiments with a range of fonts.

Make the genie emerge from the lamp

Make a set of five drawings of a genie on paper – the first should be small, the next a little larger, and so on – and cut around and colour each one. Use a digital camera to photograph a lamp with the smallest genie emerging, then the next, etc. Load the images onto your PC and play them as a slideshow – the genie should (with a little imagination) be seen to rise from the lamp!

Extending printmaking

ICT provides pupils with opportunities to extend their work in printmaking by experimenting with changes to the colours or even the composition of their prints:

1 Scan prints into the computer (or take digital photos of them).
2 Open up the image in any art and design software package.
3 Colours and tones can now be altered – or select a section of a print then copy and paste it several times to create a new pattern.

Symmetrical patterns

Create a simple pattern with reflective symmetry. Use a 'Paint' program to create a composition of shapes and colours, then use the selection tool to 'cut' a section of colour into a new shape, e.g. a butterfly's wing. Then select the existing half, copy it, 'paste' it and 'flip' it to make a reflected half.

Repeat patterns

Repeated patterns of hexagons, triangles and rectangles can inspire a range of activities in art and ICT. Constructing regular shapes using a drawing package is relatively straightforward – children can then experiment with different strategies for interlocking them to make repeating patterns.

Using the internet

One of the challenges that is almost unique in teaching and learning in the primary school is the fact that many teachers consider their pupils to be more ICT-literate than they themselves are. In no area is this issue more relevant than when using the internet. Even children with relatively limited experience of using the internet will be aware of how quickly and easily they can deviate from the virtual path prescribed by their teacher onto other, possibly less educational, avenues.

Therefore the challenge for teachers is to provide children with a structured approach to using the internet, to set challenges that require them to locate and access specific information. Inevitably this demands an amount of research on the part of the teacher – who will also be aware that information on websites can quickly date. See Chapter 7 for further reflections on using artists' work in the classroom and for a list of recommended websites for major galleries and museums.

Summary

This chapter has sought to present teachers with a clear and accessible guide to the range of practical art and design processes used in primary schools and Foundation Stage settings. While reading this chapter you may already have begun to reflect on the nature of the work produced by pupils in your classroom and in others in your school. You will most likely have noted that certain processes are carried out more frequently than others, that some processes require specialist equipment or materials that your school needs to purchase and that certain skills may need to be taught to members of staff in order to encourage and persuade them to deliver a broad curriculum for art and design.

While it may be a challenge for every teacher to master all the art and design skills that are taught to children between the ages of three and eleven, it is vital that they develop and maintain an awareness of the importance of variety and plurality in their art teaching.

It is arguable that the broader the art and design curriculum, the more opportunities there will be for pupils to develop and realize their own ideas and to experience success. A narrow curriculum can easily lead to children believing that they lack the relevant artistic knowledge and skills to make significant progress in the subject: 'I can't draw as well as her, so I'm no good at art'.

Over the course of the next three chapters you will find a range of useful information to support you in the three key areas that will enable you to effectively deliver a broad, balanced and creative curriculum for your pupils. From organizing your classroom, through to planning sequences of lessons and assessing children's learning, these chapters aim to provide you with a solid framework within which your teaching of art and design processes covered in this chapter should flourish. Through teaching basic skills, alongside children and responding to the work that children make, teachers will create and encounter real opportunities for developing creativity in the classroom. Whatever the process and whatever the ages of the children learning, the important thing for teachers to remember is that the emphasis should be placed upon teaching children to find their own unique way of responding to the challenge of making art.

Bibliography

Adams, E. (2001), *Start Drawing*. Enfield: The Campaign for Drawing.

Adams, E. and Baynes, Prof. K. (2001), *Power Drawing Notebooks*. London: The Campaign for Drawing.

Baker, J. (1991), *Window*. London: Walker Books.

Barnes, R. (1989), *Art, Design and Topic work 8–13*. London: Unwin Hyman.

—— (2003), *Teaching Art to Young Children 4–9 (Second edition),* London: Routledge

Carle, E. (1969), *The Very Hungry Caterpillar*. New York: Philomena Books.

Child, L. (2001), *I Will Never Not Ever Eat a Tomato*. London: Orchard Books.

Curriculum Online: www.curriculumonline.gov.uk

DfEE/QCA (1999), *The National Curriculum: Handbook for Primary Teachers in England – Key Stages 1 and 2*. London: QCA Publications, also available at: www.nc.uk.net.

DfEE/QCA (2000), *Art and Design: A Scheme of Work for Key Stages 1 and 2*. London: DfEE/QCA Publications, also available at: www.standards.dfes.gov.uk/schemes2/art.

—— (2005), *The Annual Report of Her Majesty's Chief Inspector of Schools, 2004/05*. http://live.ofsted.gov/publicaions/annual report0405/4.1.1.html, accessed 20 November 2006.

Eglinton, K. (2003), *Art in the Early Years*. London: Routledge Falmer.

Green, L. and Mitchell, R. (1997), *Art 7–11: Developing Primary Teaching Skills,* London: Routledge.

Herne, S. (1997), *Art in the Primary School (Policy & Guidelines for the National Curriculum)*. London: London Borough of Tower Hamlets Inspection & Advisory Service.

Lancaster, J. (1990), *Art in the Primary School,* London: Routledge

Meager, N. (1993), *Teaching Art at Key Stage 1*. Corsham: National Society of Art and Design Education.

—— (1995), *Teaching Art at Key Stage 2*. Corsham: National Society of Art and Design Education.

Morgan, M. (1988), *Art 4–11*. Oxford: Blackwell.

National Curriculum in Action: www.ncaction.org.uk.

Newland, M. and Rubens, M. (1989), *Art: A Tool for Learning*. London: Calouste Gulbenkian Foundation.

Taylor, R. (1986), *Educating for Art: Critical Response and Development*. London: Longman.

Watkins, M. (ed.) (1998), *Artworks: A Scheme of Work for Art: Early Years to Key Stage 2,* London Borough of Tower Hamlets Inspection and Advisory Service.

Williams, D. (1997), *Step by Step Art for . . . (Nursery/Reception, Key Stage 1, Lower Key Stage 2, Upper Key Stage 2)*. Preston: Topical Resources.

4 Organization of Art and Design

Strategies for organization

Ideas about learning and teaching across the curriculum as a whole, as well as in the area of art and design itself, will influence the way schools and teachers make provision for art and design in the Foundation Stage and primary curriculum. There are usually practical or educational reasons why things are organized in particular ways. It is important for teachers to find out not only about existing approaches to organization, but also to ask why – to make sure that what is in place allows art and design to be taught in appropriate ways. This will raise issues about what is appropriate, which is all-important if we are to develop a creative, questioning and educationally valid way of teaching art and design. The key to classroom organization (see, for example, Galton 1995), is *fitness for purpose*. We need to think clearly about what our educational purposes are and to make decisions about how we should organize our teaching to achieve these, ensuring that both our aims and our strategies are educationally and ethically justified.

In assessing the implications of different forms of organization we need to bear in mind that practical issues should not override educational aims. The practicalities of organizing and managing art and design in the classroom can be daunting, as it is a subject that is resource-intensive and the materials themselves can be messy. It is easy for teachers to avoid, say, getting out the pastels, for fear of the resulting smudges on clothes, hands and faces and broken pastels being trodden into the floor. However, this kind of thinking can seriously limit the range of activities which are made available to the children, with damaging consequences to their education.

Decisions about organization are an educationally significant aspect of teachers' practice: they are indicative of the way the teacher thinks about learning and teaching. This chapter presents forms of organization that are more flexible than the kind of practice to be found in some primary classrooms across the UK. It is suggested that, throughout the Foundation Stage and primary years, children should be encouraged to make choices and decisions about when and how they make art, in negotiation with their teachers, giving them ownership of their own work while acknowledging that the teacher has an important role in supporting and extending pupils' learning. This approach has clear implications for decisions about organization and these are discussed in relation to different aspects of organization. Practices and alternatives are considered with regard to the organization of timing and grouping within the curriculum. The organization of the classroom environment is addressed, drawing attention to the classroom as a learning environment, including display and resources, and the implications of a more flexible approach to organization are discussed in relation to children's learning.

Some schools are already taking advantage of the possibilities for flexibility opened up by the implementation of the Primary Strategy (DfES 2003) with its greater emphasis on personalization and on cross-curricular forms of planning, for instance. This chapter takes account of these opportunities for change. Where the suggestions in this chapter might not seem to coincide with the existing policies in some schools, they should be seen as alternative ways of thinking as a starting point for change. The chapter not only responds to current developments in national policy, but presents arguments for approaches to the organization of art and design that are consistent with the nature of the subject and with children's development.

The more flexible approach to learning and teaching in art and design that is proposed in this chapter reflects the existing character and principles of much early years (Foundation Stage) educational practice in the UK (see, for example, Fisher 2002, Chapter 3). The Foundation Stage curriculum (QCA/DfEE 2000) clearly endorses activity that is initiated by children in the context of their play activity. All the principles discussed in this chapter apply to the early years, as well as to Key Stages 1 and 2, especially in relation to rich provision for play-based learning.

Organizing learning in the early years – Foundation Stage

The organization of learning in the Foundation Stage around the six areas of learning (see QCA/DfEE 2000 and Chapter 2) is generally perceived as distinctively different to that of the later stages. Much of the activity in the early years classroom is child-initiated: for instance, play is a central feature. The child-led approach accommodates the ways in which young children learn. (For more information on this see, for example, Fisher 2002, Chapter 3.) As a consequence, there are less likely to be rigid divisions between subject areas in the way children's activities are organized in early years settings: the activities which children engage in during their play provide them with opportunities for learning through a range of curriculum areas. Some of these activities will provide opportunities for creative development, and some of that creative development will be in areas that we think of as 'art and design'. It has to be remembered however, as has been pointed out in Chapter 2, creative development occurs across the whole curriculum. Even the area of 'the arts' – which constitute the area of learning designated as Creative Development in the Foundation Stage Curriculum Guidance (QCA/DfEE 2000) – includes a wide range of aspects such as dance and drama, music, story and poetry. Given this form of curriculum organization it is unlikely that an early years setting will have a rigidly structured timetable. Much of the learning will take place through free play or other child directed activities; some will be more structured or adult initiated – for instance, the adults might decide to encourage a response to an experience such as a story or a topic that the teacher and children are exploring. In successful early years classrooms, individual children will have at least some degree of choice about what they do and when they do it.

In the early years, a classroom that is well provided with materials to draw, paint, model, construct and use computer software will be one in which children's learning in this area can flourish. This will depend on the teacher providing the opportunity – the time – for the children to use the materials. It will also depend on the right kind of teacher support: teachers need to respond to the initiatives the children take. The best kind of interventions do not direct the children or deflect them unnecessarily from their preoccupations, but, through appropriate interaction, will stimulate and extend their thinking. Conversation, on equal terms with the child but skilfully sustained by the teacher to introduce, explore and challenge ideas, will enable the child to build on what they already know. This will occur more readily in a classroom where the natural free-flow of children's self-chosen activities is encouraged, for at least part of the time, and this will depend on how the classroom is organized – again, in terms of time and resources.

Some provision to promote creative activity in art and design can be a more or less permanent feature of the classroom. For instance, a painting area with easels and a rich choice of painting materials, which children are allowed to move into freely and in which they can access the materials themselves, allows them to pursue interests and ideas as they occur in their play and thinking. When time, space and materials are to hand children can freely transform their thinking from other modes into the mark-making mode (see Pahl 1999). The same applies to construction activity. Variety is important. Richness in provision can be enhanced by equipment and media that are selected for the different representational possibilities that they offer and challenges that they present – for example, empty cardboard boxes of all sizes and shapes and swathes of fabric offer one range of possibilities; shiny paper, sticky backed coloured plastic and scissors or paper, liquid paint and straws to blow through offer another. There is scope for being adventurous: for instance resistant materials and appropriate do-it-yourself tools (wood, saws, hammers and nails) can be used even by young children with appropriate adult supervision. Working outdoors with large scale materials and ephemera that can be found in the environment present yet another set of possibilities.

A guiding principle for a well-organized early years setting is that it should aim to stimulate and extend children's activity, curiosity, persistence, creativity, imagination, investigation and powers of representation and communication. This is a way of working that should be extended into the later primary years as well.

Organizing learning at Key Stage 1 and Key Stage 2

Organization of art and design within the curriculum – timing and grouping

One of the first points to consider in terms of organization is how the school structures the curriculum within the school day, week and year and how art and design is incorporated.

Fixed timetables

In contrast to early years settings, there is often a structured timetable in place for pupils at Key Stages 1 and 2, with a designated time for art and design lessons each week, so that the whole class engages in art and design at the same time, especially at Key Stage 2. Why is this? It may be for practical reasons: for example, limited art and design resources may need to be shared around the school, in which case there may be a staggered system of art and design sessions across the school, allowing little flexibility for the individual class teacher. It may be that a specialist teacher supports or teaches art and design, moving from class to class to teach whole-class lessons in the subject. Alternatively, it may be that the school has adopted a single subject, whole-class approach to teaching across the curriculum, perhaps on the grounds of ensuring that each curriculum area receives an appropriate amount of time and attention and that there is a clear subject-based focus to the teaching. This is more of an educational reason, related to particular views about learning and teaching. Sometimes, when an initiative in one area of the curriculum is introduced, it can have an effect on the way other curriculum areas are structured and, in the UK, 'core-subjects' (English, mathematics and science) often take precedence over other areas in this respect.

Sometimes, there are neither practical reasons, nor sound educational ones, for the way that art and design education is fitted in but, rather, habitual ways of working that reveal some questionable assumptions. For instance, sometimes the only opportunity given to the children to 'do art' is on a Friday afternoon. What might this suggest? That art and design activities are undemanding in nature, are activities that are suitable for a time when children might be tired? That they are a 'treat' with which to reward them at the end of the week? That they are undemanding in terms of teaching so are an easy option for the teacher at a time when he is looking forward to the weekend? Or that art and design are less important aspects of the curriculum that can be left until all the more important teaching and learning has been done? Clearly, if this is the kind of thinking that underlies some persistent ways of organizing space for art and design on the timetable, then it needs to be recognized and challenged.

These forms of organization are tending to give way to more holistic or cross-curricular approaches to planning.

'Blocking'

In contrast to the prescribed timetabled slot, some schools have adopted an approach in which subject areas receive blocks of time. For instance, a single subject may be prioritized over others for a certain length of time, up to about a term in duration, allowing children to focus on a particular area. This can be across the whole school, or for individual classes – perhaps with each class in turn adopting this approach. This approach can also impose restrictions on teachers' freedom to make the longer-term decisions about how to organize their teaching, but is often justified on educational grounds of continuity and progression, rather than for reasons of practicality. For instance, it allows children to extend their thinking in a particular area without the interruption to attention and motivation that can occur when children move from subject to subject. It enables them to undertake more sustained projects with the intention of engaging them at a deeper level. Sometimes, schools have 'art and design weeks' when the whole timetable is given over to this area of the curriculum. Again, this sort of whole-school decision may not suit all individual teachers, but it can bring the same sort of educational benefits. It can also have practical advantages: organization might be streamlined for teachers when resources and effort are concentrated in a short, intensive period of study and there are opportunities that might otherwise be difficult to create, such as the short-term involvement of an artist in residence available to work intensively with the children over the course of a week, either in school or in the artist's studio. However, there are issues around entitlement, balance, continuity and progression that need to be considered if the concentrated block of time is the only art and design teaching the children get in any term or year.

A more flexible approach?

It is worthwhile considering whether there are educational reasons for alternatives to the timetabled approach. When there is a prescribed 'slot' for the art and design lesson each week, it does mean that teachers can focus their planning and interaction on specific aspects of teaching and learning in art and design, and can model processes and skills for the whole class. However, it also means that children are expected to develop ideas and work creatively within a prescribed time frame. Furthermore, it allows no flexibility in how long a child can spend on their art and design work. If a child has an idea or the inspiration to make art and design at other times of the week, then this may not be possible under these kinds of arrangements. Similarly, children may feel the need to spend much longer developing their ideas than is made available in the timetabled session. We have to ask: How important is it for children to have control of their own art and design activities? Is it important for children to learn that, in art and design, ideas can be self generated and developed, and, as teachers, should we acknowledge that this may be time intensive? The process of developing and realizing ideas is a central aspect of art and design and can only be learned through engaging in it. The National Curriculum emphasizes that children should learn to research and develop their own ideas – yet the restrictive nature of a weekly time slot can make this difficult.

It may be that teachers decide collectively that a more flexible approach should be adopted as a matter of principle and that it should become a whole-school policy to allow children to make decisions about when, and for how long, they engage in art and design activities, reintroducing the patterns of learning that the children may have been more familiar with in the Foundation Stage. Clearly there will be practical issues such as those around resources and the organizational implications around specialist provision – if that exists – which will have to be addressed. If we prioritize flexibility, then this may mean that there need to be more art and design resources. Ways and means of achieving this have to be found, otherwise decisions about what is important in the teaching of art and design are compromised – children may have control over when to do art and design activities, but if they do not have the necessary resources for their purposes then the gains can be outweighed by losses. The role of the specialist teacher is called into question, if there are no longer fixed 'lessons' for them to teach. Furthermore, there may well be implications for other areas of the curriculum, in that too much time may be spent on art and design and too little on other areas, or vice versa. It may become more difficult to maintain the balance of learning across the whole curriculum. If different children spend different amounts of time on art and design then this balance can be even more difficult to monitor as it will differ for individual children. All these implications must be borne in mind if this more personalized approach is adopted, but they are essentially practical difficulties which, in themselves, do not invalidate this way of working. It is important that educational aims determine what kind of experience children have, rather than practicalities.

Flexible grouping – small and whole-class groups

Within a flexible form of organization, the teacher maintains the option of having the children working in groups, including the whole class working together, if and when this is needed for particular purposes. Children can be encouraged to work in small groups, perhaps allowing them to come together to explore shared interests or to work together on a collaborative project. Again, in a flexible environment, such group work can be responsive to child-initiated ideas as well as being initiated by the teacher. There are also times when it is useful for the teacher to work with the whole class together, for example, to demonstrate particular processes or techniques, or to focus everyone's attention in a session on observational drawing. A whole-class session, of the kind recommended for literacy hour plenaries, can provide a good opportunity for discussion and reflection. Having the whole class involved in evaluating the work of other artists or pupils' work, for example, can provide differing perspectives and ideas and an opportunity for pupils to learn from each other, providing new avenues for developing their work. Arguably, it can also help to raise the status of art and design to give regular, whole-class discussion time to it.

Cross-curricular links

Although it may be a more complex way of organizing time for art and design, a flexible approach can be educationally advantageous in other ways. For instance, there may be more opportunities for teachers and children to integrate learning in art and design with learning in other areas of the curriculum. Where there are no predetermined time slots for art or maths, for example, the teacher has the freedom to decide that the research that children have been engaged in for their study of tessellation in maths can be related to patterns in Islamic design, resulting in children learning how to make repeated patterns through printmaking activities as part of a combined mathematics and art and design activity. It also allows for children themselves to respond to topics in other curriculum areas in art-focused ways. If children know that they can choose to pursue art and design activities when they have been inspired by their work in History, for example, then this can increase levels of motivation and they may also benefit from making conceptual connections around the topic. For example, a child may become particularly interested in the design of buildings in the Tudor period through a history topic. She may be motivated to investigate architectural features of buildings in the environment, perhaps comparing different styles and addressing the question 'how does the style of buildings of a particular era relate to the way of life?' by looking at the evidence from the points of view of several curriculum areas, perhaps history, art and technology. In terms of learning through art and design, the teacher could make it possible for the child to make sketches; to ask further questions and do research about styles and design ideas in other artefacts from the same era; to make a portfolio of different features and be able to make comparisons and talk about them; to learn more about shape and line in the architectural design of the period and to design their own buildings. The links between curriculum areas must be thought through carefully. There is renewed interest in cross-curricular teaching in UK primary schools but teachers need to be wary of the pitfalls that were discovered in 'topic' based teaching in the past. It is all too easy to lose sight of the forms of enquiry, concepts and skills that help children to make sense of any experience. Learning about the natural environment, for instance, from the point of view of a scientist or a geographer involves accessing and interpreting evidence in particular ways that are not the same as the ways in which an artist might interpret and appreciate it. The scientist might be interested in the process of erosion on soil and will carry out observations and experiments to discover how this happens. From an art and design perspective, different sorts of enquiry would be appropriate, such as investigating the patterns formed by erosion or using the environment in imaginative ways to inspire new ways of looking at it and understanding it (the work of David Nash or Andy Goldsworthy provides an example). Different concepts, processes and skills are developed through each distinctive form of enquiry and it is important that children are introduced to them, to extend the ways they might make sense of the world. It was all too prevalent, in integrated teaching in the past, for the 'art' element of the curriculum to be little more than providing opportunities for illustrating history topics, say, with scant attention given to learning the ways of understanding, processes, concepts and skills specific to art and design. To avoid this, teachers need to remain aware of the ways in which different forms of enquiry contribute to knowledge and understanding in particular ways and to ensure that in the pursuit of more meaningful contexts for children's learning they offer opportunities for all children to be able to learn in all these ways. It is for these reasons that cross-curricular teaching is perhaps best thought of as learning *through* different subject areas.

Organization of art and design within the curriculum – content of children's learning

As suggested above, classroom organization is influenced by both principles and policy. In the preceding section it has been shown that if it is important for children to make decisions about their art and design work then this has implications for how the subject is organized. When we introduce flexibility in terms of timing, however, there are also implications for the organization of content. The example given above illustrates this. It shows how flexibility in terms of timing has inevitable consequences for flexibility around *what* children are learning.

As already discussed, one of the advantages of allowing children to decide when they involve themselves in art and design activities is to enable them to respond to their own ideas. Clearly there are implications for the teacher's planning of content if the children are encouraged to do this. Different children will have different ideas at different times. For example, some children may get immersed in building clay models of landscapes investigated on a school trip, while others may be less interested in this and more interested in pursuing their printmaking ideas, inspired by a tessellations project. Again, the practical difficulties emerge. How can the teacher ensure that all the children are acquiring the range of concepts, skills, processes, knowledge and attitudes that it is important for them to learn, and that they are statutorily required to teach? It is not only in planning that difficulties might arise. When children are engaged in different activities, it is more difficult for the teacher to make sure that they interact with and challenge each child sufficiently to ensure that they are developing their understanding, abilities and knowledge, or that the pupil's learning is being extended.

One way of monitoring the content of the children's learning and making sure that they can be adequately supported and challenged is to encourage the children to negotiate their plans with the teacher. This helps the teacher to plan to accommodate the children's interests while bearing in mind what they need to learn. This brings us to the area of assessment. Clearly, the increased open-endedness of a more flexible approach also has practical implications in relation to the assessment of children's learning. To inform their teaching, to know what kinds of intervention and support are appropriate, the teacher needs to know what the children are learning. When children are following up their own lines of investigation and making their own decisions about what they should make, this can be especially challenging for the teacher. It is not as straightforward as checking what the children are doing against the criteria for the lesson objectives. The teacher will need to be aware of, and responsive to, what different children are doing and this will mean an open approach to evidence of learning in a variety of different areas of understanding and skill in art and design at any time. A further organizational issue, then, is the challenge of keeping careful records on a more individualized basis than in a whole-class teaching situation.

Record keeping

There are two kinds of record that are useful to keep. The teacher needs to know the kinds of artwork that each child has undertaken, in a factual way, so that she has a record of the concepts, processes, skills, techniques, knowledge and attitudes that the child has had the opportunity to acquire. The teacher needs to ask herself 'What opportunities does this activity present?' Experience in different media is fairly straightforward to monitor, in that the skills necessary to work in the medium successfully can be easily identified. It is more complex to ascertain the kinds of concepts the child will be able to acquire from a particular project or piece of work. Often this will be dependent on the direction in which the child takes the work, so the teacher will need to be responsive to what the child is learning as the work develops. This is where the second sort of record keeping comes in. As well as identifying what the activity offers, by way of learning opportunities, the teacher needs to assess what the child has actually learned. If the teacher adopts the more flexible approach to organization, it is most important that the records of each child's learning are kept in a systematic way to keep track of individuals' development. One way of doing this is to have a chart of the children's names drawn up with a space next to each name so that comments can be written alongside the name. Another way is to have sheets prepared for each kind of activity that the child is likely to encounter, with some of the key learning opportunities that it offers (the particular concepts, processes, skill, techniques, knowledge and attitudes). If this approach is used, however, it is important to focus on what the child actually learned, as this may not match what is presented on the record sheet. There would need to be a space for recording any further learning that had not been anticipated in advance. Using a computer-based approach to these methods of record keeping means that records can be readily accessed and amended or updated.

A more open approach is to keep portfolios for each child where a variety of evidence of learning can be kept, including the teachers observational notes, notes on conversations between child and teacher that provide evidence of significant learning, the child's self evaluation of their own work, and possibly examples, or at least photographs, of the children's work. A digital camera is very useful here, and digital records of the children's work can easily be kept as part of a computer-based system, by scanning in examples of work, for instance, and can be a useful part of whatever form of record keeping the teacher chooses to use.

The organization of the classroom as a learning environment

In all Key Stages, the way the classroom is organized indicates how the teacher thinks about learning and teaching. A classroom which opens up, rather than closes down, the possibilities for creative and imaginative work is one where children will be motivated to make art. This will be one where the surroundings and the available resources give children ideas and set them thinking, and is a place where there is room to investigate and develop those ideas in an orderly, independent way. The physical arrangement of the classroom is central to this and requires careful thought and management.

Organization of resources and the physical environment for learning in Foundation Stage classrooms

In an environment where much learning is play-based, it's important that materials, equipment and provision are very varied and are selected to develop a wide range of concepts and skills, and that this range of resources is made available in a way that inspires children and encourages them to use what is provided in their play. A well-equipped Foundation Stage classroom will have a wide range of mark-making media, perhaps in a designated drawing and writing area, with a good selection of different kinds of paper. It will have construction materials and model-making materials such as dough, Plasticine and clay. There will be materials for printmaking, digital media such as cameras and simple drawing software loaded on the computer, materials for work with textiles and found materials that provide representational possibilities. Building blocks of different kinds provide opportunities for imaginative, three-dimensional thinking as does outdoor play equipment. There will be a rich supply of books that includes picture books of the work of artists as well as story and picture books that can stimulate children's imaginations and the role play area might at times have a specifically art and design related theme, such as a poster shop, a pottery, a jewellery studio, a face painting stall, an art materials shop or an art gallery.

The resources should be well maintained and preferably stored or placed in the classroom in a systematic, consistent way so that children can access them for their self-directed activities. Most teachers will make a range of basic activities available on an everyday basis, such as mark-making, model-making, construction and painting. Sometimes teachers will wish to create new interest or focus on particular ideas or skills, so will often put certain equipment out for the children to use and may rotate the use of different media over time so that children's interest in it is renewed. Advance preparation is essential, and all the equipment required for a particular activity will need to be ready, especially if the activity is to be undertaken independently by the children. In addition, adult-initiated activities, such as introducing the children to a new process or skill might require the use of equipment that might not be regularly available, such as printing inks. These will need to be stored in places known to all the adults working in the classroom.

The classroom and the outdoor area need not only to be exciting learning environments but need to accommodate active children in safety, so the way that furniture and space is arranged needs to be carefully considered. An early years classroom that encourages exploration and experimentation is likely to have different areas and tables for different activities and open spaces available for larger-scale projects. Thought will have been given to the positioning of easels, for example, and access to the sink.

The whole classroom should be an aesthetically pleasing environment.

Organization of resources in Key Stages 1 and 2

What are the practical implications of a more flexible approach to organization of the art and design curriculum for the organization of resources in Key Stages 1 and 2? Clearly, when there is one session a week, art and design resources would not be needed for the rest of the time and can be used by other classes or stored away. When the teacher has preplanned the content of the art and design sessions he can prepare the materials and resources that are required for a particular session. A more flexible approach, on the other hand, requires that the resources are ready and available at all times. When children are negotiating their own plans around their art and design activity, this requires a wide range of resources to be at hand. This can create practical problems in that more resources are needed and will have to be continuously maintained. One solution to the management of resources is to encourage independence and responsibility on the part of the children. They can be taught how to look after the materials and where they are kept. Simple rules and procedures can save a lot of time and frustration: for instance, children should know that paintbrushes should not be used for glue. (It is easier to have this simple rule than to be continually washing glue out of paintbrushes.) Systems can be created by the children, together with the teacher, around care and storage of resources so that all the children know how to find what they need, to use it well and to return it to the appropriate place. For this reason it is a good idea to have things stored at child level with items sorted and clearly labelled. It is important to consider the special needs of children in the class. Children who use wheelchairs, for instance, will also need to be able to access materials and equipment so they should be stored at an appropriate height. Obviously, safety must be taken into account and certain items will need to be kept separately, perhaps in a locked cupboard to which the teacher alone has access. (A list of resources that might be used within the art curriculum is provided in the Appendix.)

Space and furniture in Key Stages 1 and 2

In the context of flexible organization, it makes sense to have an 'art and design area' in the classroom, where art and design activities can be going on continuously and where the necessary equipment and materials are stored. The children can move into the art and design area to work as and when this is negotiated with the teacher. Some classrooms are supplied with a variety of furniture for different purposes. High tables in the art and design area allow children to stand up while working and to move freely around larger-scale work or work which requires more equipment. Similarly, it is useful to have some easels available so that children can place their drawing and painting at an angle that suits them and enables them to stand back from their work to view it. An art and design area that is rich in resources and children's ongoing and displayed work can create a classroom environment that conveys a sense of excitement about art and design, in contrast to the classroom that has no more evidence of art and design activity than an impoverished sink with a pile of dirty paint pots beside it. Sadly, some classrooms, especially those that are in 'mobile classrooms', sometimes even lack the basics of sink and water supply. This is a challenge, but not insurmountable. While they are not ideal, buckets and containers can be made continuously available and furniture arranged to create a space, so that children are provided with a classroom that carries positive messages about 'wet' activities. Having said this, space in any classroom is often at a premium and it can take considerable ingenuity on the part of the teacher to arrange it so that it is flexible and reflects the teacher's priorities and principles about learning. It is all too easy to revert to the 'newspapers on tables on a Friday afternoon' for the whole-class art lesson, but there are more imaginative solutions in any classroom.

ICT

ICT resources – computers, cameras, videos, etc. – can be regarded as tools in art and design or as media in their own right. Children can use the computer or a camera as a way of trying out ideas before developing them in another medium, for example, or for producing art or design work in digital or photographic form. Within a flexible form of organization, computers would need to be available to children within the classroom and they would need to be instructed in the use of appropriate software. In order for computers to be used as a learning tool it is good practice for them to be available for use inside the classroom as well as in a separate computer suite. Portable equipment, such as PC tablets, mean that children can use the computer at their table. In all cases, of course, the positioning of computers needs to be considered to avoid contact with water. There is no reason why children should not also have easy access to cameras and video cameras if they understand how to use and take care of them, in the same way as other more expensive equipment.

Paper

A plan chest enables paper to be stored flat and to be sorted into different kinds. It is a good idea to recycle as much paper as possible. Different 'grades' of recycled paper can be stored in different places: for instance small 'flat' scraps and off-cuts can be placed in a flat drawer, whereas crumpled pieces can be put in a larger drawer, a box or one of the containers on wheels which are found in classrooms and can be pushed underneath tables. Since there are at least some children who enjoy sorting things out in almost every class, there should be help at hand in managing paper resources in this way! Off-cuts can be re-sorted as they gradually degrade, through use and re-use, from large flat pieces, to smaller scraps and finally to crumpled bits.

Equipment storage

There is a wide range of different equipment that is desirable, if not necessarily always available, for art and design work in the primary classroom. This varies from the more expensive, such as stoves for batik and silk screens for printmaking, to the more ordinary, such as charcoal and needles. The teacher will need to keep a close eye on more expensive items, even if children are taught how to access and use these appropriately themselves. It may be that they need to be shared across the school in which case they may be kept in a central storage area or cupboard. But children (and teachers!) need to know of their existence so that they can be used when it is appropriate. If the children are unaware that the school has certain equipment, and if they are not introduced to it and shown the techniques and skills for using it, then their choices for their own art and design work are limited, unnecessarily. For the more commonplace items, it is a simple matter of common sense to decide on the most appropriate container (if required) and the location for these. Classroom furniture suppliers' catalogues have a range of effective storage units, sometimes mobile, for instance, with open containers of different sizes for different sizes and types of equipment. The advantages of these are that each item can be assigned its place, and is open to view for ease of identification and replacement, and the unit can be moved to the appropriate place in the classroom. There can be different trolleys or units that contain all the necessary equipment for particular media and processes, such as printmaking, for example, that can be stored or wheeled around as they are needed. They are particularly useful in Foundation Stage classrooms in that children can explore the range of resources stored in the many containers. For instance, a unit with all sorts of found objects and scraps and different joining and fixing materials from paper clips and masking tape to hole punchers and treasury tags will stimulate construction activities. The features of these units mean that children can access equipment independently. If the school can't afford this kind of storage, then tins and boxes, or the usual kind of 'tray' storage, found in most classrooms for children's belongings can be used for art materials and labelled and located with children's independent access in mind.

Tools such as scissors and saws are best kept in some central but safe location where the children have easy access to them, can help themselves and return them. One method, which teachers commonly use for storing tools safely and checking where they are, is to keep them on a pinboard, with hooks for each tool and a drawing on the board around its outline that shows visually which item goes where. In the Foundation Stage classroom, the teacher would need to make a judgement as to whether tools could safely be made available in this way – or whether they would need to be provided by an adult. Often, some basic training can ensure safe use and allows the children more independence.

Recycled media and conservation of materials

Teachers and children can make their own collections of cereal and food packets (be aware of health and safety issues around these) and other recycleable materials for use in three-dimensional work. It pays to go further. There are increasing numbers of recycling centres which will have available a supply of recycled waste material suitable for use in creative work in the classroom. This can be enormously useful and inspirational. Arrangements differ, but usually, for a nominal cost, teachers can obtain a wide variety of consumable materials (usually obtained by the centre from factories of various kinds) ranging from ribbons, buttons, fabric off-cuts and small, plastic items to cardboard tubes, acetate sheets and large rolls of paper. These are treasure houses which should be explored by any teacher who has ever seen the possibilities in a discarded cardboard box! These materials need not be thought of as ends in themselves, but as a resource to be manipulated to help children achieve their ideas. Storage of larger amounts of scrap material may become difficult, however, so it needs to be kept under control. Regular visits to the centre, perhaps with particular purposes in mind, and thoughtful organization of the material, so that it is available in manageable quantities, can be very valuable. Remember that too much clutter in the classroom can turn useful and exciting materials into uninspiring junk.

Materials should not be wasted, for environmental reasons as well as cost. Children should learn how to use materials and equipment wisely and economically. A useful rule of thumb is to ensure they use the right tool for the right purpose. If they have been taught how to care for everything they use, then they should be able to work independently without too much waste. Again, simple procedures, such as adding darker colours to lighter ones and keeping lids on liquids can help. If children have mixed large quantities of interesting colours, make sure they know they can be returned to the art corner, in pots, for other children to use, rather than washing them down the sink. Again, children's own, common-sense ideas can be used to help develop routines and their understanding of the issues around sustainable use of resources that they may have developed in geography can be applied in art and design. Learning how to organize their own workspace is important in helping to conserve materials, as well as helping them to produce work of quality. Children can be taught how to ensure that materials are ready to hand before they start, and are placed on the work surface in a logical way. It can be difficult for anyone to keep their work area under control so the teacher clearly has a role in helping children to develop their own organizational skills.

Children's work

Work in progress can be a problem, in any classroom. There may always be paintings that are drying and models that are half built around the classroom. Again, designated storage places are a solution. A rack (available from suppliers for the purpose) for drying paintings and prints is a good idea. These are designed so that pieces of work can be inserted on individual racks which pull down to form a stack. Alternatively, a line strung across the room (out of reach of children and adults passing underneath) can be used to peg up the work until it's dry. Children's work should be displayed on the walls of the classroom or around the school (see p. 99).

Organizing other adults

Teaching assistants can be very experienced and may be very knowledgeable about art and design, as can parents who give voluntary help in the classroom. Clearly, where there is the need for supervision of an activity with a small group, particularly one where specialist equipment is being used, a classroom assistant or a parent can be invaluable to make sure that children use the equipment appropriately and safely. Teaching assistants are often assigned, and sometimes specifically employed, to work with children with special educational needs and some are trained in this. Again, this is a great help to both children and teachers. The teacher needs to ensure that when supervising an activity the other adult does not take over from a child, whether or not they have special needs, but, rather, supports them where necessary. There can be a fine line between supporting and taking over. Where practical support is required, children's independence should be encouraged and children should always 'have a go' themselves. Explanation or demonstration can help, but it is better for the adult to help clarify a problem so the child can solve it. In terms of developing ideas, the adult needs to be particularly sensitive to the kinds of intervention that are appropriate. As a general rule, the work should always be the child's own. A further point that must be borne in mind when organizing provision of adult support for children with special needs, is that these are the children who need to work with a qualified teacher as well as a teaching assistant. It is all too easy to assume that a child is making adequate progress without the teacher's support, especially in a subject like art and design that is perhaps deemed more recreational or a less important aspect of a child's learning. This applies to other children as well. A further implication of a flexible approach to organization is that a teacher may be tempted to over-rely on teaching assistants to support art and design activities in small groups, while the teacher works on other activities that are running alongside. Again, it is most important that the qualified teacher provides sufficient input in art and design.

There is no doubt that having a team of people in the classroom, that includes the teacher and teaching assistants, is helpful in managing, organizing and maintaining equipment and materials and in putting up displays. To maintain good relationships it is a good idea for teachers and teaching assistants to democratically devise systems together that work for all who need to manage them, rather than the teacher having a top-down approach towards a teaching assistant. The teacher can provide guidance, where necessary, in terms of educational priorities, principles and practice.

Practising artists are widely available to work in classrooms, either for a one-off project or on a more permanent, ongoing basis. Sometimes, artists are given a studio space, if there is an empty classroom, in return for working with children. Artists in school can be very inspirational – information on who is available and how to organize visits can usually be obtained from local arts organizations or regional arts councils. Similarly, local artists are often willing to have groups of children visit them in their studios.

Displays

If children are to see that their ideas are valued and that they are continuously being encouraged to implement them, then the classroom as a whole should reflect the work that is going on in it and should give messages that children's own work is always in progress. In this sense the classroom should be 'alive' with art and design. This is more than last year's carefully mounted display, put up for the Ofsted inspection and hung on to because it shows excellent work. This has its value in the short term – it provides a model of the quality of work to which children can aspire. But it can become stale and does not necessarily provide ongoing inspiration. An alternative is to create a workshop atmosphere where children know that newly completed work is always being displayed, and that work in progress is out on view where children can see its changes and development. Any form of display is demanding of the teacher's time, even with the help of classroom assistants, but, if nothing else, should be weighed up carefully against competing priorities. The classroom should also be rich in artefacts and experiences which will be a source for children's ideas. Again, these should change frequently. If they can sometimes be connected with other interests that the children are developing, one interest can inform another. Thus, a table display might contain a range of objects with different surfaces and textures, alongside a range of materials for collage, at the same time as children are investigating the idea of friction in science. The scientific concepts they acquire as they ask questions about the surfaces of materials and undertake experiments may help them to think about the variety of surfaces in their environment, which in turn may help them to include varied and contrasting materials in their art work. The art work, in its own way, may 'say' something about the contrasting qualities of surfaces. The presentation of the materials in the classroom environment acts as a stimulus to the children's thinking, which is deepened through discussion with the teacher.

Displays of the work of other artists and designers, both original (if possible) and in reproduction, provide children with examples, not of styles to imitate but of the ways that other artists have worked (see Chapter 7). If used by the teacher and children as a resource for learning, rather than as 'wallpaper', they can give children insight into the sorts of strategies that different artists use and different sorts of solutions to problems that they themselves might encounter in their own work, as well as an ability to experience and critically appraise the work of others.

Display in the classroom is a topic about which whole books have usefully been written (see, for example Cooper *et al.* 1996). It is often associated with the art and design curriculum, but effective display, that contributes to children's learning, is a cross-curricular issue. However, it does require aesthetic sensibilities on the part of those who create it, and children can extend their learning in art and design through being involved. At the time of writing, new legislation has been introduced in the UK aimed at reducing teachers' workloads and handing over responsibility for certain tasks to classroom assistants. Putting up displays is one of those tasks, but it is important to note that *planning* the display remains the responsibility of the class teacher, even if, physically, the actual assembling of the display is done by someone else. This is important: if display is valued in terms of its contribution to children's learning, then planning educational display should be part of the teacher's role.

Summary

Organization may appear to be simply a practical matter, but every decision that a teacher makes will be influenced by what they understand about children and their learning; teaching and the nature of art and design as an area of practice and knowledge. This chapter has introduced some of the ways in which different ways of thinking might affect teachers' organization. It has highlighted the implications across different aspects of organization. In particular it has addressed the organization of art and design within the curriculum and the various aspects of the organization of the learning environment, including resources and materials, other adults and displays. In all respects, what teachers do is a matter for their professional judgement, drawing on all the knowledge and understanding that this entails. While guidelines and suggestions can be useful, it is important for teachers to see organization as an aspect of teaching that is shaped by aims and values as much as any other, and should be subject to reflection, review and development.

References

Cooper, H., Hegarty, P., Hegarty, P. and Simco, N. (1996), *Display in the Classroom: Principles, Practice and Learning Theory*. London: David Fulton.

DfES (2003), *Excellence and Enjoyment: A Strategy for Primary Schools*. Nottingham: DfES Publications.

Fisher, J. (2002), *Starting from the Child (2nd Edition)*. Maidenhead: Open University Press.

Galton, M. (1995), 'Do you really want to cope with thirty lively children and become an effective primary teacher?', in J. Moyles (ed.), *Beginning Teaching, Beginning Learning*. Buckingham: Open University Press.

Pahl, K. (1999), *Transformations: Meaning Making in Nursery Education*. Stoke on Trent: Trentham Books.

QCA/DfEE (2000), *Curriculum Guidance for the Foundation Stage*. London: QCA/DfEE.

5 Planning Art and Design

The aim of this chapter is to provide teachers with strategies for effective planning in art and design. It highlights the need for flexibility and continuity in teachers' planning, and suggests that children should engage in a range of creative activities that offer opportunities to develop specific practical skills. It emphasizes the importance of sequencing lessons in a way that makes learning in art and design meaningful for children and provides three examples of sequences of lessons, each of which could be adapted for teaching children between the ages of 3 and 11. With thanks to Caroline Corker, Rachel Chatten, Louise Iacovides, Alistair Lambert and Tanya Ying for practical ideas.

Many teachers have a positive approach towards teaching art and design. They have high expectations of their pupils; they want them to develop their knowledge and understanding of the subject, to learn a range of technical skills and they want to see the emergence of work that is interesting and original. Art lessons can often, however, end in disappointment: pupils become confused about what they are supposed to have learned, resources turn out to be inappropriate and the work produced is repetitive and lacking in ambition. This chapter is set in the context of Foundation Stage settings and primary schools in the UK, although the perspective it provides may be equally relevant to teachers working in other countries.

Elsewhere in this book you will find discussion of the status of art and design at the Foundation Stage and in the primary curriculum; it is assumed here that art is a subject more vulnerable than most to the pressures of the timetable and that the time available for teaching it is restricted. Teachers are consequently faced with a choice: either to accept that art is a marginalized area to which scant attention should be paid, or to ensure that the limited amount of time allocated to the subject is used effectively. The former option will lead to art lessons that offer few opportunities for pupils to develop skills and leave little room for creativity; the latter requires more thought, planning and reflection but will be the first step towards providing pupils with a valuable art education.

The planning process: long-term, medium-term and short-term

The aim of providing a balanced curriculum underpins strategies for long-term planning for art and design at the Foundation Stage and at Key Stages 1 and 2. A successful long-term plan is one that, over the course of a Key Stage, ensures that pupils are provided with opportunities to access all aspects of the National Curriculum for art and design. In theory, establishing a long-term plan for art and design in a school should be relatively straightforward, but in practice the process is often hampered by a lack of continuity in the leadership of the subject. A system that is initiated by one subject leader can easily break down when the role is transferred to another, which can result in a fragmented experience of the curriculum for pupils.

Effective planning involves reflecting upon children's progress and feeding this information forward, a process that begins at the Foundation Stage: 'Good planning is the key to making children's learning effective, exciting, varied and progressive. Good planning enables practitioners to build up knowledge about how individual children learn and make progress. It also provides opportunities for practitioners to think and talk about how to sustain a successful learning environment' (DfES 1999). Early years practitioners plan across the six areas of learning in the Foundation Stage including Creative Development. There is likely to be more integration of creative/art and design activities at this stage in pupils' learning; in fact, practitioners will seek opportunities for creative activities to reinforce learning in other areas of the curriculum.

Planning for art and design at the Foundation Stage should therefore take account of opportunities to:

- carry out observation of individuals or small groups;
- develop vocabulary associated with the creative activity;
- make informal assessments of children's progress in creative activities.

Box 5.1 Long-term Planning – Year 5

Autumn Term

Recording Skills: Self-portraits; figure drawing. Studying proportion, shape, line, tone, texture, expression, movement, light and shade.

Comparison of Styles/Recording: Tudor portraits – detailed drawings of costume and jewellery – paper collage.

3D/Craft Skills: Design and make a Tudor picture frame.

Comparison of Styles: Study portraits by Hans Holbein; investigate symbols/objects of identity.

ICT Produce a digital image based on multiple images of 'myself'.

Spring Term

Shape and Pattern: Design based on a family of objects – leaves, shells, bones, fruit. Focus on shape, form and tone – light and dark, tints and shades.

Recording Skills: Using designs to experiment with painting techniques: watercolours, block/ready-mix, acrylics.

Colour Work: Investigating artworks concerned with colour, tone and texture: Paul Klee, Sean Scully, Fiona Rae.

Comparison of Styles: Making work inspired by Fiona Rae's paintings – exploring a range of approaches to composition.

Colour Work: Making large-scale, group collages using torn paper.

Collage: Developing work in sketch books: observational drawings from objects of interest collected on visit to park: identifying details of objects to make abstracted pieces.

Summer Term

Recording Skills: Use sections of drawings as starting points for designing and making press prints. Develop press prints into two/three colours.

Colour Work: Scan press prints onto computer and crop sections to experiment with copying/repeating/rotating patterns.

Shape and Pattern/ICT: Study examples of Bridget Riley's paintings to extend possibilities of print and ICT work.

Comparison of Styles: Using ICT to develop experimental approaches to collage.

Pictorial Composition: Reflect on strategies for developing compositions through use of collage.

Box 5.2 Medium-term Planning – Year 5

Focus: Greek Gods in paintings from the National Gallery

Week	Key learning outcome	Activity
1	To understand that looking closely and talking about a work of art can help us to understand it	'How to be an art detective': looking for clues in Tintoretto's 'Origins of the Milky Way'
2	To understand that symbols were widely used in classical paintings	Identifying symbols in Tintoretto's painting; devising a set of personal symbols
3	To develop skills – moulding, carving, adding texture – that will support the designing and making of a clay pot	Select and incorporate symbols into a personalized clay pot
4	To recognize the potential of a range of recycled materials for use in sculpture	Use newspaper, card and recycled materials to make a collection of 3D figures inspired by those in Tintoretto's painting
5	To develop observational drawing skills – focus on composition	Make drawings of the 3D figures assembled into groups
6	To extend experiments with figure compositions through use of ICT	Make collages of figures in new compositions combining digital photographs

A successful long-term plan is one that, over the course of a Key Stage, ensures that pupils are provided with opportunities to access all aspects of the National Curriculum for art and design. In theory, establishing a long-term plan for art and design in a school should be relatively straightforward, but in practice the process is often hampered by a lack of continuity in the leadership of the subject. A system that is initiated by one subject leader can easily break down when the role is transferred to another, which can result in a fragmented experience of the curriculum for pupils.

A medium-term plan will typically summarize the learning across a term or half term, breaking down the knowledge and skills identified in the long-term plan into accessible sections. Approaches to medium-term planning vary from school to school. While the QCA scheme of work (2000) is widely used in UK schools as a source of both long-term and medium-term planning, teachers should be aware that, unlike the National Curriculum, it is not compulsory to follow the scheme and that many schools opt to pursue their own plans. Alternatively, a keen subject leader or classroom teacher may either adapt the scheme to suit the learning needs of the children in their school or class, taking what is needed and rejecting the remainder, or supplement it with additional materials. Several examples of medium-term plans are explored at the end of this chapter.

Short-term planning is carried out on a weekly or daily basis. The amount of short-term planning that is required of each class teacher will depend largely on the quality of the medium-term planning that is in place. For practical purposes, it is assumed here that teachers have received from their subject leaders a similar amount of planning as that provided by the QCA scheme: that is, that a range of learning opportunities and practical activities have been suggested, but that teachers have some freedom and flexibility as to the sequence in which these learning opportunities are provided to the class and how the children will be taught.

Box 5.3 Short-term planning – Year 1, Autumn term

Learning intention	**Context**	**NC/FS**
To explore approaches to mark making	Exploration of materials	2q, b, 5a, c

Key questions	**Activity**
Looking at Leon Kossoff's charcoal drawings	To make five experimental drawings using a different drawing tool for each one
How can you describe the way the charcoal has been used?	
What could you do to make tones look darker/lighter?	
What would happen if you put one colour over another?	
How did I get this effect? (smudging, etc.)	
What happens when you press harder/softer with the materials?	

Resources and organization	**Differentiation**
Set out on five tables: charcoal; oil pastels; watercolours; chalk pastels; coloured pencils.	**Extension:** Challenge children to use drawing materials to match a selection of specific textures
Ask children to investigate a range of drawing media and to produce patterns using the different media. Explain they need to find out the best thing to use when they draw their self-portraits next week.	**Support:** Green group to work with Ms M. investigating effects of spraying watercolour over oil pastel
Plenary Ask children to describe similarities and contrasts of different materials	

ICT opportunities Investigate the range of drawing tools on 'Colour Magic' – challenge each other to create specific effects using a limited range of tools.	**Cross-curricular opps Science:** Properties of materials
	Multicultural opps: Explore contrasting fabrics and patterns from different cultures

Box 5.4 Short-term planning – Year 2

Number in Group 30

Time/duration

1 hour 20 mins

Main activity

Paintings/collages inspired by photographs of buildings

Place in Sequence

This is Lesson 1 of a three-part lesson sequence

Learning Intentions

Children will look at an artist's work critically.

Children will develop painting or collage skills through using a photograph of a place as a basis for an abstract piece of work.

Pre-activity Organization

You will need:

- The large prints of Sarah Morris's paintings from the practical resource folder.

- The PowerPoint disk and an interactive whiteboard or computer.

- The photographs of buildings from the practrical resource pack.

- Paper, paints and different materials for collage.

Individual Provision

Encourage children who are less confident to look at the shapes of the buildings and base their work around those shapes. Have the PowerPoint presentation for children to look at again if they have not fully understood the ideas behind the paintings. Ensure there is a good mix of ability in each group.

Assessment

Children will have clearly expressed ideas on the art and worked as a group to form ideas on the subject matter, techniques used and use of colour. Children will have produced a piece of work based on a photgraph; the finished piece should show understanding of shape and diferent use of colour to the subject matter.

Timing	Teaching Strategies	Children's Activities
10 mins	Introduction What we will be doing – looking at art, then making a piece based on the ideas we have seen. Divide the children into groups.	Moving to groups as directed by teacher.

30 mins	Give each group a large print and ask them to answer the questions written on the board: • How do you think this piece of art was made? • What do you think it was based on? • How does it make you feel? • How do you think the artist felt when they made it?	**Group discussion.** Children should be observing the colours and the shapes in the artwork.
	Ask each group to feed back to the class. Explain that Sarah Morris painted the pictures using household gloss on large canvasses and that they were based on buildings and places in cities. Tell each group what their painting was based on.	They should have ideas on how it was made and what the subject is. Children should be working as a team with all members of the group contributing.
40 mins	Introduce the practical activities by asking the children to choose painting or collage. They will be using a photograph of some buildings to inspire their own work.	Deciding which materials they want to work with, paint or collage. Looking at their photograph and finding the shapes. Drawing the outline of the shapes onto the paper. Using paint or collage to fill these shapes.
	The children can work in pencil first but encourage them to mark out a guide of the shapes and lines of their drawing then fill in with colour. While they are working, talk to children individually about what they are doing and ask them questions on why they are using certain colours and shapes.	
	Plenary: explain that next lesson this topic will be continued and we will look at the work made this lesson.	
	Let the children feed back their feelings on the session: did they enjoy looking at the art? How did they find the activity? Have their feelings about Sarah Morris's work changed at all?	

Differentiation

Differentiation in teaching art and design is an interesting issue and one that is worth reflecting upon. The principle that underlies the practice of planning different activities to meet the needs of individual pupils or groups of pupils is that all children should be able to satisfactorily achieve a specific aim. For example, a group of children in a maths lesson should be set questions that are challenging yet manageable for them, and in such quantities that ensure that they are able to complete a particular task. An alternative approach would be to provide each child in the class with an identical sheet of questions, each progressively more difficult than the last, thereby ensuring that only the most able pupils succeeded in completing the entire task. Art lessons offer opportunities to experiment with different and potentially valuable strategies for classroom organization.

While it is perfectly understandable why teachers choose to divide their class into ability groups for some subjects, they should also be aware of opportunities to experiment with different organizational structures, and there are some creative ways in which teachers can reorganize learning in art lessons (or lessons in other subjects, such as design and technology). Even young children placed in a particular ability group are often quick to develop a perspective on the position of their group in relation to other groups in the class. Art lessons offer opportunities to break with routine, and children who would perhaps normally work in separate groups for learning in the core areas may quite happily work alongside each other. Teachers might reflect on the potential benefits of such an arrangement in terms of the social cohesion of the class: it may come as a surprise to teachers that many of their pupils *do not know each other*. Mixed-ability teaching can offer children opportunities to reconstruct a sense of their own individuality within the class – an afternoon spent at Red Table can do wonders for a lost soul hitherto marooned on Green Table. It is easy to overlook the extent to which children learn from each other as well as from their teachers.

Children in the early stages of learning English can be vulnerable to assumptions that their language limits their potential across the wider curriculum. Art lessons offer opportunities for such children to redefine themselves in their own and others' eyes. Once again, the teacher who is sensitive to such issues will organize the classroom in such a way that maximizes opportunities for these children to work alongside others that they might normally, for however sound reasons, be separated from.

While it is often the case that those children who succeed in other curriculum areas are also confident in their learning in art and design, there will exist in most classrooms children who will come to see art as a subject that provides them with a unique opportunity to demonstrate their abilities. Furthermore, the uniquely visual nature of art and design means that, even in a short space of time, such a child is able to produce work that his teacher can hold up as a positive example to the rest of the class. A child who struggles to keep pace with literacy lessons might rarely have the opportunity for his/her work to be shown in such a way. If such opportunities are taken, teachers can successfully influence the subtle dynamics of the classroom and provide valuable support for children in need of it.

Having said this, some children will need extra support when engaging with particular processes and practices. The visual nature of the subject can ensure that, when children do experience problems in a particular aspect of it, the evidence can be difficult to conceal. This is one of the key benefits to be gained from teachers engaging in practical work on initial teacher education courses or as part of INSET training: working alongside colleagues can quickly alert one to the difficulties of a particular process, an experience that will prove useful when it comes to reassuring disappointed pupils. A key theme that underlies all these approaches to differentiation is *flexibility*, a theme that is explored below.

Planning: flexibility and continuity

Flexibility is a quality to be admired in teachers, one that is nothing short of essential. Unfortunately, teachers' capacity for flexibility is often constrained by medium-term plans that propose sequences of six or seven weekly lessons. Documents such as the National Literacy Framework prescribe a level of detail in planning that some teachers think should be matched by other subjects. Plans that identify specific learning outcomes for a sequence of six or seven lessons may appear to be evidence of a thorough approach to the subject, but they will discourage teachers from allowing pupils to evaluate and develop their work, to adapt it in the light of what they have learned and to assume some ownership of the direction in which their work is heading.

It is understandable that teachers feel that in order to ensure that prescribed learning outcomes are met by the end of term, then they should encourage their pupils to progress quickly from one planned activity to the next, almost regardless of whether pupils have finished their work, understood key teaching points or had opportunities to revisit areas that need further exploration. The restricted time available for art and design can easily lead teachers to encourage pupils to move swiftly from one art activity to the next, thereby unintentionally giving them the impression that to repeat an activity would be a retrogressive step.

This is an approach that contrasts sharply with that employed by many artists. Were you to visit a retrospective exhibition of an artist's work you would expect to see evidence of continuity in their work. An artist may produce work over a prolonged period, and across a range of media, but a consistent style and recurrent themes are likely to emerge. Indeed, many artists are recognized and respected for their ability to formulate and refine individual and original styles of working. Similarly, children need time to plan their own ideas, to think about ideas, to return to ideas (and even, like many artists, to appropriate ideas!). They need time to practise the skills that they are taught; they need time to make mistakes, to learn from mistakes, to respond to feedback and to learn from other artists' work.

Teachers should consider building in to their plans some space for flexibility. Rather than aim to guide their pupils towards specific learning outcomes written weeks in advance, they should move towards establishing an environment that encourages opportunities for children to reflect on what they have achieved so far and to make their own plans for future work. An activity proposed for the sixth week of term cannot realistically be planned until the outcomes of lessons taught in the first two or three weeks have been evaluated. Teachers who doggedly follow a sequence of planned activities will often miss important opportunities for pupils to develop and demonstrate their creativity, and may risk creating situations in which they try to steer pupils' work in one direction while their pupils are pulling in another.

Evaluating art and design activities

So how are teachers to identify art and design activities that provide appropriate and challenging learning experiences for their pupils? Some valuable lessons can be learned from teachers' own memories, both happy and unhappy, of the art education they received as a child. This is not to propose that our strategies for teaching and learning art in the twenty-first century should depend mainly upon our memories of cheerfully sticking cotton wool to Christmas cards as five-year-olds, but to suggest that it can be informative to reflect on what made art enjoyable – or unpleasant – for us as children and how those experiences might impact upon our practice as teachers.

My own recollections of one sequence of art lessons taught to me as a young child are particularly depressing. In the first week of term each member of the class was presented with a book that depicted costumes through the ages, each page of which was illustrated with a line drawing of, for example, a man and woman appropriately attired for a day out in Ancient Rome. Each week we were asked to make a copy of one of these line drawings and then to colour it in, a task that carried us through to the summer term. Worryingly, I have no recollection of an inclination to rebel against the tedium of these lessons. I simply assumed that my teacher knew best and that the objective of this repetition would eventually be revealed.

What, in retrospect, have I learned from this experience? To not underestimate the extent to which pupils think that their teachers are experts and that whatever they say is right. A child that has experienced relative freedom using a range of materials in the early years may be unlikely to complain when later restricted to pencil and paper. After all, the teacher knows best and, as far as the child is aware, this is what art lessons are like from now on. If teachers are to encourage their pupils to develop and maintain a positive attitude towards art and design, the nature of the practical activities in which they engage is crucial. Consider two examples:

Example 1

I once observed a student teacher teach an art lesson in which she provided each child with a photograph of a mask made by another child and a set of instructions on how to make the mask. The instructions are paraphrased here: 'Trace the template on page 11 and cut it out carefully. Cut out two holes for the eyes, one for the nose and one for the mouth. Cut a sheet of A3 paper into narrow strips and use glue to stick them to the top of the mask . . . .' However impressive the accompanying illustration of the mask looked, it was almost inevitable that, given the prescriptive nature of the instructions, each child would produce a mask almost indistinguishable from those of his/her classmates.

Most young children want to get things right and avoid making mistakes, and, for those children who are able to follow instructions carefully, this activity offered opportunities for *getting it right*. For those who struggle to follow directions, however, the opportunities to make mistakes outnumber those for success. By choosing to teach this activity, a teacher risks giving his/her pupils the message that making art is: (a) about carefully following instructions; and (b) about producing work that looks the same as that made by the person next to you. Some children will excel at activities such as this. Others will struggle and eventually succeed. A few will fail. They will make too many mistakes and their work will look nothing like the example in the book. It is possible, however, that the work made by this last group will be far more individual and interesting than those 'correct' examples made by other children – but this is a perspective that would be difficult to explain to the child who holds up to his teacher a soggy, misshapen mess of cardboard while his classmates skip happily out of the classroom wearing identical disguises.

Example 2

Figure 5.1 Now draw a picture

The activity that produced this drawing (Figure 5.1) is equally problematic, but for contrasting reasons. It is not difficult to visualize the context in which this drawing was made. Chikira has finished writing towards the end of her literacy lesson and, having been invited by her teacher to 'now draw a picture', has made a simple illustration of the text. As you will imagine, she was provided with little in the way of guidance or support while making the drawing, the results are very similar to drawings she had made before and the finished piece prompted little if any feedback from her teacher. A teacher who asks for a drawing, yet provides little guidance and makes few responses, risks giving pupils the message that drawing is not an activity worthy of discussion, but simply something that children can do when they've finished their 'real' work.

Furthermore, children whose experience of drawing consists largely of making illustrations for their writing may be unprepared for a more demanding task in an art and design lesson. Let's imagine that Chikira's Literacy lesson is followed by a lesson in observational drawing, in which she and her classmates are encouraged to pay close attention to detail in their drawings. How will her teacher explain to Chikira that the level of skill previously demonstrated in her illustration is no longer sufficient? That the depiction of her teacher that was acceptable in the morning is regarded as hopelessly inaccurate in the afternoon?

There is an argument to be made that children's experiences of producing artwork independently, with a minimum of guidance from a teacher, are an essential factor in their development. However, teachers would be well-advised to review a selection of drawings produced by their pupils, and to consider whether the selection demonstrates a balance between independent work and work that has, to some extent, been directed by the teacher. This is not to argue that children should be banned from illustrating their stories, but encourages teachers to think twice before advising children to 'now draw a picture!'

So what constitutes an appropriate practical activity in art and design? Our aim should be to plan activities that are neither completely teacher-led nor entirely child-led, activities that are neither too prescriptive in nature nor left entirely open to interpretation. At times teachers will be required to demonstrate new techniques and skills to children, and at other times children will be encouraged to respond to a particular experience or stimulus in their own individual ways. The challenge we face is to teach these techniques and skills while simultaneously providing opportunities for children to work creatively and with individuality.

Sequencing lessons in art and design

This section provides three examples of sequences of art and design lessons. Through discussion in the classroom teachers should encourage children to reflect on the progress they have made with their practical work and to identify ways in which ideas may be extended. By being aware of a number of ways forward, teachers can more confidently support children in the choices they make and be more able to challenge and enthuse them. The sequences are intended as examples of possible routes that may be taken by children as they engage with a range of ideas and processes and it is not intended that they should be followed literally. Teachers who submit detailed plans for six or more lessons at the start of a term may be reluctant to change those plans midway through the sequence; it is important to retain some flexibility. An effective sequence of lessons is one that has sufficient flexibility to enable the teacher and children to reflect on the outcomes of the early lessons and to make subsequent plans, rather than one in which the sixth lesson is planned before the first has been taught. Teachers should try to provide opportunities for pupils to make decisions about their work and for these decisions to influence the direction of subsequent work.

A flexible approach to medium-term planning has more in common with the ways that 'real' artists work. Artists will generally work across several pieces simultaneously, allowing one development to influence the next in a natural, organic way. Few would set themselves targets and deadlines that may involve abandoning an unfinished painting because their timetables say that they should have moved on to printmaking by now. Similarly, children need to be allowed time to pursue particular aspects of their work that they find interesting and challenging. The following sequences of lessons make several references to artists' work. Relating children's work to that made by artists is not essential, but in doing so teachers can encourage children to see that the work they are making is part of a tradition and that the problems they face and the decisions they make are often similar to those faced by artists (see Chapter 7). In each sequence, it is assumed that art lessons are a weekly feature of the classroom – though carrying out similar sequences across a shorter period of time will give children opportunities to really engage with the ideas they are exploring.

Sequence 1: Newspaper clothes

'But how can we teach art when we've got no paint, no pencils, no ink and no money . . .?' In the long term, there is no substitute for adequate resources for art and design, and teachers should endeavour to provide children with quality materials. If old worksheets are the only drawing paper provided by teachers, pupils will soon get the message that their work is not highly valued. There are times in the school year, however, when money is tight and the call goes out for recyclable materials. Making newspaper clothes is an activity that requires minimal resources, can offer children opportunities to express their imagination and ingenuity, to extend their repertoire of practical skills and to improve their ability to work as part of a team. It is also, specifically, a *design* activity as well as an art activity, as there are certain practical targets that must be met – for example, the clothes must be wearable if not durable – if the piece is to be considered a success.

Figure 5.2 Newspaper clothes

This activity can be carried out with children of any age, from the Foundation Stage to Year 6 and beyond, although teachers' expectations will vary according to the age of their pupils. Pupils are asked to work in groups of three; each group is given a supply of newspaper and masking tape and asked to make an outfit of clothing for one of the group to wear. Teachers may, if they wish, provide further resources or, if they prefer, provide fewer. (Allocating strictly limited supplies to pupils could alter the emphasis of the activity significantly, possibly prompting further innovation from the pupils.) This activity is an example of one that is neither wholly teacher-led nor entirely child-led. Teachers should make clear to children that they are working within set parameters – they are restricted to using only newspaper and masking tape – but that within these parameters they have the opportunity to create pieces of work that are individual and unique to them.

The key to success with this activity is to ensure that children are well prepared for it. Making newspaper clothes at the beginning of a sequence of lessons may be an enjoyable experience for the children, but if they are to fully benefit from the experience then they will need to bring to the activity a range of relevant knowledge and skills. Let us assume that the activity will form the second in a sequence of lessons. What should be taught in the first?

Box 5.5 Newspaper clothes

Week 1: Investigating materials

The first lesson in the sequence should provide pupils with opportunities to investigate the properties of newspaper as a material to work with. A sheet of newspaper has specific qualities and can be changed in different ways. It can be torn randomly or cut precisely; its volume can be increased by scrunching it lightly, pages can be taped together or shredded into strips while symmetrical patterns can be cut into folded sections; its strength can be increased by rolling it tightly (these rolls could be plaited into rope-like lengths for extra strength). Some of these options will occur to children immediately. Others will occur to them if they are given time to explore the qualities of the newspaper without having the additional pressure of having to use it to construct something. Groups could each be assigned a different area to investigate, and results could be shared at the end of the lesson. The children may not have made anything that they want to keep, but they will have gained valuable experience of working with the materials.

This first lesson could be compared to a Literacy task in which pupils are asked to gather an appropriate range of vocabulary for, say, a story about a haunted house. It is not necessarily a creative task, but one designed to enable children to refine and share their skills in ways that will be useful to them for the subsequent task.

Week 2: Newspaper clothes

Before the second lesson, children could be invited to gather source material, such as photographs from magazines, to influence their designs. Teachers may wish to identify a specific theme, perhaps one linking with work in other curriculum areas, as having too many options to choose from can be as difficult as having too few. Designs could be shared and refined through brief preliminary sketches, tasks could be allocated to individual members of each group. Children should focus on applying the skills and techniques practised in the previous session to constructing an outfit based on a shared design. Learning to work effectively in groups can be a challenging task for young children. Teachers are faced with a choice: should children be left to work individually in order to avoid potential disagreements and conflicts? Or should they be offered opportunities to develop the necessary social skills through working as part of a team?

Week 3: Newspaper clothes – revisited

Few teachers will be brave enough to hand in a set of plans that says 'Same as last week', but there are times when repetition is appropriate. Some children will feel that they have achieved what they set out to do in the activity, while others may have been frustrated. Seeing the work made by some groups may help others clarify their ideas and want to persevere. Should they not be offered a second chance?

⇨

Weeks 4, 5 and 6: Possible directions

At this point the teacher should reflect on the progress so far. What is it about the activity that has engaged the children? What aspects of the lesson need to be built upon and in which areas do pupils need further experience? Possible directions could be:

Textiles

Keeping the theme, but changing the materials: focus on the process of constructing an item of clothing from a flat pattern – explore the use of symmetry in drawing and cutting patterns.

Three dimensional work

Keep the materials, but changing the permanence of the work. Papier maché is a useful medium for sculptures, built from plastic bottles, cardboard rolls and boxes (ensure that structures are sound before adding papier miaché, as the weight of wet paste can crush fragile arrangements. This can be effectively achieved using gummed, brown paper tape).

Drawing

Figure drawings – models posing in newspaper clothes, class arranged at desks in a semicircle around them. Experiment with short poses of two to three minutes, with pupils in 'action' poses; encourage children to work quickly from the head down to the feet, to sketch lightly with their pencils, to keep detail to a minimum (and to not worry about erasing mistakes).

Collage

Encourage pupils to make a collection of images found in newspapers and to reassemble them in ways that either form a narrative or an abstract image.

Cross-curricular links

Plan and present a fashion show based around the newspaper clothes. Over the course of a week, the theme of the fashion show could permeate many areas of the curriculum, possibly leading towards a presentation in a school assembly:

Numeracy	Calculations of the 'costs' involved will need to be made
Science	Explore the different qualities of the materials that the clothes could be made from
Literacy:	Write lyrically descriptive reviews of the clothes
History	Research what a fashion show might have looked like 100 or 200 years ago
Geography	Research the similarities and differences between clothing worn in a selection of countries
Music	Compose or select appropriate music to accompany the fashion show
RE	Explore the significance of particular items of clothing in world religions
D & T	Change the emphasis of the activity – challenge children to create the tallest or strongest structure, using strictly limited quantities of newspaper
ICT	Design a poster to advertise the fashion show, incorporating photographs or drawings – or bring the project full circle by creating a newspaper!

Sequence 2: Maps and routes

Artist Alistair Lambert has worked on a range of projects in schools and other community settings and (as someone whose route to the classroom has studiously avoided teacher education) offers a fresh approach to planning a sequence of lessons. Many of his ideas, such as a sequence of collages inspired by Scalextric tracks, have a playfully investigative quality to them. Ideas that may initially appear sketchy are allowed to evolve from one lesson to the next, with children engaging in a range of interrelated practical activities. For the project outlined here, Alistair was invited to use the theme of 'Safe routes to school' as a stimulus for a sequence of lessons taught to a Year 5 class. 'The project followed on from a number of lessons that had explored issues around transport and the environment,' explains Alistair, with the aim of the subsequent art activities being 'to explore through visual means various ideas related to travel, maps and the way we locate ourselves in our environment'. The sequence of lessons was not planned in its entirety in advance. After each lesson, Alistair reflected on the outcomes that had emerged and considered ways in which children's ideas could be extended through subsequent activities. While many teachers will be required to submit plans for a sequence of lessons before teaching the first, the way in which the planning for these lessons evolved over the course of a few weeks offers teachers an alternative perspective on the process.

Box 5.6 Overview of five lessons

Week 1: Maps

Children were each given a photocopy of a map of the local area and asked to colour in first their route to school, then areas and buildings on the map according to a key of their own design. The children's work quickly shifted away from a geography exercise and towards investigating shape and colour. Children were encouraged to look within the maps for abstract shapes created by the grids of the streets and for patterns that emerged through the repetition of these shapes; these were then emphasized by colouring individual sections.

Week 2: Collages

The compositions that emerged from the first lesson formed the starting point for a collection of collages. The details of the original maps were now simplified into areas of flat colour, bringing to mind the work of artists such as Matisse, whose influence can be seen in the collages that the children produced in the second session. The collages were then combined to form a large-scale piece that resembled less a map, more an abstract painting.

$\Rightarrow$

Week 3: Buildings

The grid formed by the collection of collages led children towards making a three-dimensional version in the third session, in which they made sculptures inspired by familiar buildings in the local area. In another context, clay could have been used to make the sculptures, though Plasticine was used in this case. A technique similar to that used to make coil pots was used to make the structures, which were displayed together to make streets and squares, thereby taking the two dimensional patterns of the collages and translating them into three dimensions. The immediacy and colour of the sculptures also related closely to the collages made in the previous lesson.

Week 4: Routes A to B

The theme of roads and routes was returned to with a lesson that featured a playful collage activity inspired by Scalextric tracks and motorway junctions and based upon straight lines, curved lines and bridges. Using paper strips cut from templates, children worked in pairs to create interlocking networks of lines that curved around and crossed one another in a way reminiscent of model roads and railways. The activity highlighted the way in which small decisions – turn left, turn right, go straight ahead – can combine to result in complex networks of lines that form intriguing compositions. Although children had the freedom to experiment with their compositions, they were asked to ensure that each piece contained a line that entered their frame halfway along each side of the rectangle. This would eventually enable the individual collages to link directly with each other when displayed, to form continuous routes that children could then rearrange in endless permutations – another opportunity for them to engage in making decisions about the appearance of their artworks.

Week 5: Body maps

In the following lesson the children returned to the initial theme of mapping an area, only this time using their body shapes as the basis of large-scale collage pieces. Inspired by diverse images – an ancient Greek frieze depicting a group of runners, photographs of footballers cut from newspapers – children lay across grids of coloured card, struck dynamic poses and drew around the outlines of their bodies. The resulting figures were cut out and placed over grids of identical sizes but contrasting colours, creating striking pieces that referred back to the grids that framed the maps used in the first lesson. Finally, image editing software was used to reduce photographs of the children posing to silhouettes that went on to form the basis of permanent sculptures displayed along the perimeter fence of the school.

These lessons succeeded in engaging pupils' interests and creating a range of interesting and experimental artworks, and there are several aspects of the work that teachers will find interesting and useful to consider when planning their own sequences of lessons. The activities described are carried out by individuals, by groups and by the whole-class with small, individual pieces of work combining together to form large-scale, whole-class displays. Children were offered opportunities to develop their teamwork skills through a range of activities that often blurred the boundaries between art and design and game-playing.

The lessons required a minimum of resourcing: the materials used in the sessions are inexpensive and can be found in almost any school. The skills that children developed during the lessons were not related to drawing or painting – the most frequently taught areas of the curriculum at Key Stages 1 and 2 – which provided opportunities for children lacking confidence in these areas to work happily alongside their more 'able' classmates. In contrast with many art lessons, the children worked with equal levels of enthusiasm and it was hard to identify work made by those regarded as having a talent for the subject.

While the lessons used the starting point of children's own first hand experiences of their local area, it also prompted them to develop their awareness of the abstract qualities of the environment. Artists are often credited with an ability to see things differently from other people; perhaps this apparent attribute might more accurately be described as a facility for finding the intriguing in the everyday, for retaining a curiosity about the visual world that many of us acquire as children and lose as adults.

Sequence 3: Abstracting from the landscape

In some respects the third sequence of lessons featured here relates to the second, in that children are encouraged to experiment with compositions that relate to the visual world, without attempting to replicate it. The sequence offers opportunities to engage with a range of art processes, and takes as its starting point images of natural forms in the landscape, such as rocks, trees and coastlines. At any point in the sequence, teachers might choose to share with children examples of work by artists who have used landscape as a stimulus for experiments with abstraction – the St Ives' artists (Ben Nicholson, Barbara Hepworth, Patrick Heron, Peter Lanyon, etc.) would be an ideal reference point. Remind children that these artists evolved their own unique artistic styles through experimenting within their work and reflecting on the results. Encourage them to follow these examples by experimenting with new techniques and striving to make pieces that are individual to them.

Box 5.7 Overview of six lessons

Week 1

Begin by showing children images of a landscape – they may be paintings, drawings or photographs, the landscape may be familiar, strange or imaginary (or even real, if a visit can be arranged). Ask children to identify features of the landscape, then to identify shapes within the landscape, naming regular shapes and describing irregular ones. Provide children with a choice of drawing materials and a choice of paper and ask them to make drawings, not of the whole landscape but of some of the shapes to be found within it. These shapes need not be drawn in the sequence in which they can be seen, but can be reordered, overlapped, enlarged or reduced. Older children can be encouraged to look for *negative* shapes – the shapes that emerge from between objects.

⇨

Week 2

The second session offers children opportunities to experiment with composition and scale through making collages based on their drawings from the previous lesson. Paper or card shapes can be cut or torn to represent the features of the landscape, and children could collaborate on group projects by combining their individual pieces. If children have visited the landscape in question they could incorporate into their collages some natural materials found at the site. Children should be reminded that they are not making representations of the scene, but compositions inspired by it.

Week 3

In this lesson children can explore composition through making paintings based on their collaged shapes. Before the lesson laminate a selection of the children's card shapes and ask children to choose several that they want to use in their paintings. These shapes can then be used as templates to be painted around, repeated, combined together, overlapped, etc.

Weeks 4, 5 and 6

The paintings made in Week 3 could be extended into several areas:

- Paint card shapes inspired by the compositions and assemble them into reliefs by using card boxes as supports to separate each layer (see Frank Stella's relief pieces)
- String prints – string stuck onto pieces of card, then inked up and printed – offer children opportunities to make linear abstract compositions inspired by their paintings, and to experiment with pattern through repetition and rotation.
- Use a paint program to recreate a section of a painting before selecting a smaller section of the image, then copying, pasting, repeating and reflecting it.

The sequences of lessons described above could provide starting points for your work with your own pupils, and they are included as examples of *possible avenues to be explored* rather than models to be emulated. It's hard to teach children to be creative – but through thoughtful planning we can provide settings in which creativity can flourish. One key way that we enable this is to reflect carefully on what we say to children when they are engaged with making their work – the suggestions we make that aim to challenge them and to develop and extend their work This is a subject that is explored in the next chapter.

Summary: planning checklist

1 Plan activities that are a balance between being teacher-led and child-led – a display featuring 30 identical pieces of work teaches children that art is all about making work that is the same as your neighbour; conversely, leaving children to work alone with little or no guidance will lead them to assume that art is simply something to fill the time between less trivial pursuits.

2 Identify the key learning points of a scheme of work – what you want your pupils to experience, to understand and to be able to do as a result of the lessons – and emphasize these points in discussion with the children.

3 Try to ensure that your sequences of lessons include opportunities for creative and skills-based activities, as well as opportunities to learn about a range of aspects of the art and design curriculum.

4 Avoid predetermined outcomes: evaluate the activities in published resources and adapt where necessary.

5 Offer children a range of materials to use in their work, while simultaneously restricting their options – too many options can be as paralysing as too few. Build in opportunities for the children to acquire skills and techniques in using the materials and to understand the processes involved.

6 With the children, reflect on the work they are making and be prepared to think sideways – don't rush to move on to the next step that was planned weeks before.

7 Offer children a choice of scales to work on. Do not underestimate the importance of this! Imagine a visit to a gallery and consider how disappointing it would be if each painting you saw was the same size. Children are used to working on A4 sheets of paper in exercise books, and may assume that the same rule applies to art until challenged by the choices available.

8 Provide sketchbooks in which children can plan ideas, gather resources and carry out individual investigations.

9 Be prepared to teach the same lesson twice. You would not expect to be able to deal with a particular learning point in a single literacy or numeracy lesson – the same should apply to art and design.

10 Try to ensure that across the year you provide opportunities for children to work on individual, group and whole-class projects.

11 When organizing groups in the classroom, make sure that art is not always the 'other' activity, with the children left to work independently – this can suggest low expectations

12 Ensure that the art area in your classroom has a changing collection of visual materials as well as practical resources.

13 Don't be disheartened by the lack of space on the timetable for art and design. Perhaps it is better to have too little time to carry out all our ideas rather than having too few ideas to fill the time available.

14 Finally, treasure individuality: while we encourage children to write their names on their work before being placing it on the drying rack, ideally they wouldn't need to – it would be instantly recognizable as belonging to them and no one else.

Bibliography

DfES (1999), *Planning for Learning in the Foundation Stage*. Sudbury: QCA.

—— (2005), 'Art and design 2004/5 annual report on curriculum and assessment' e-publication www.qca.org.uk/15722.html, accessed 25 May 06.

—— (2000), *Art and Design: A Scheme of Work for Key Stages 1 and 2*. Sudbury: QCA.

Assessing Children's Learning in Art and Design

6

Chapter Outline

Assessment is often regarded as one of the most problematic areas of teaching and learning in art and design. Perhaps more than in any other area of the curriculum, it is difficult for teachers to maintain an objective approach to responding to children's artwork; all teachers will bring to this area experiences and preferences that are likely to shape their responses. This chapter explores reasons why we assess children's learning in art and design and examines the range of forms of assessment that a school may have in place. It addresses a number of issues surrounding assessment in art and design, and offers teachers practical advice on strategies for providing constructive feedback to pupils about their work.

Issues surrounding assessment in art and design

While the assessment of children's learning in the core subjects of the National Curriculum has maintained a high profile in recent years, and teachers are accustomed to levelling children's work in English, maths and science, there has been relatively little support provided for teachers wanting to assess children's learning in the Foundation subjects. Furthermore, works of art – whether made by small children or famous artists – can be especially difficult for teachers to assess. We all have a subjective approach towards art and design, our own preferences and prejudices, and making decisions about the success of a particular work of art is a very personal process. It can be very difficult to put one's own preferences to one side and judge a work of art purely on its own merits.

There is arguably little consensus of opinion on what constitutes a 'successful' work of art, whether it hangs on a wall in a classroom or at Tate Modern. For artists – and children – this can constitute an exciting and challenging concept: there is no right or wrong way, and if that is the way they want their work to look, then no one can persuade them otherwise. For teachers, however, this can be confusing and frustrating. *How do I respond to this piece of work? Is it good or bad? Do I like it or dislike it? What could be done to improve it?* A pupil presenting a painting to her teacher may assume that she knows best, yet the teacher may have little confidence in their own opinions and be reluctant to provide criticism or advice. Personal taste may play a role in the process of responding to a piece of work, but teachers' knowledge and understanding of the subject should also inform their responses. In other words, a teacher may not particularly *like* a painting that a child brings to him, but he should nonetheless be able to suggest ways in which it might be improved.

Many teachers feel that their own lack of technical expertise inhibits them from making constructive criticism of children's work. Teaching children how to draw is perhaps the most common reservation teachers have about teaching art and design. Many adults claim, almost with pride: 'I can't draw' – but few would boast of a similar inability to spell accurately, or an incapacity for understanding addition and subtraction. Initial teacher education courses in art and design should provide student teachers with practical experiences of making art using a range of processes.

However, it is important that teachers understand that they do not themselves have to be skilled artists in order to teach the subject effectively. Not many Year 6 teachers would be able to outrun every member of their class, yet most still consider themselves qualified to teach them athletics. What children need from teachers is not impressive demonstrations of their own technical skills, but evidence of genuine interest in the children's work and an awareness of ways in which it might be improved.

Furthermore, although its presence in the National Curriculum is firmly enshrined, art is a subject still viewed by many children as a leisure activity, rather than an area of learning in which they need to be challenged to make progress. Indeed, it is arguable that much of the artwork made in primary schools is made *outside* of art lessons. In Chapter 5 we reflected on some of the issues arising from inviting a child, having completed his writing, to 'now draw a picture'; the invitation implies that the real work – the writing task – is now complete, and that it's time to relax. A teacher who asks a child for an illustration, yet provides no guidance and makes no response to the subsequent drawing, risks giving pupils the message that artistic activity is not worthy of discussion, but simply something that children can do when they've finished their 'real' work.

To understand one of the key issues surrounding assessment in art and design, it may be helpful to make a comparison with strategies teachers use for assessment in literacy. Although teachers wish to inspire their pupils to produce written work that is creative and original, they are also simultaneously aware of the importance of adhering to the conventions of writing: using capital letters and full stops, writing in full sentences and paragraphs and spelling individual words correctly.

A child who presents his teacher with a painting of his family that features a haphazard arrangement of misshapen heads, oddly proportioned limbs and indefinable splodges of colour may be perfectly content with the representations that he has made and may regard the departures from reality in his painting as fully intentional. However, it is also possible that he is frustrated by the fact that the figures in the picture bear only a fleeting resemblance to his loved ones and that he actually anticipates from his teacher some thoughtful and practical advice on how to represent them in a more recognizable light.

The teacher, therefore, may well hesitate before responding to the painting: what does this child want to hear – or need to hear? There are no spellings to correct, no paragraphs to be delineated, no handwriting to refine; would it be unkind to point out that, were his mother to walk through the door looking like *that*, the child would be horrified? Would it not be easier to praise him gently with a 'well done'?

Quite often, the responses that teachers make in such situations are intertwined with the learning outcomes they have identified. Some teachers are guilty of beginning an art lesson with too fixed an idea of what the likely outcomes should be, and are inclined to welcome from their pupils only examples of work that meet their restricted expectations and that will not stand out from the crowd of work selected for the classroom display. A little Picasso, proudly presenting a distorted portrait of his mother to his unsuspecting teacher, would have been unlikely to thrive in such a situation.

Displaying children's work is a natural conclusion to the process of assessment; sadly, some schools have a policy of only displaying children's work if it is aesthetically pleasing or appealing. The rationale of many classroom and corridor displays is to enhance the appearance of the school and to help create an attractive learning environment rather than to reflect the range of learning taking place in art lessons. This is not to suggest that schools seek to ensure that a certain proportion of work displayed should be bleak in nature or bland in appearance, but it raises issues of equal opportunities – should the same children, most likely those with a talent for or inclination towards art, always have their work displayed, while the efforts of others are consigned to obscurity?

Why do we assess children's learning in art and design?

So, given that the assessment of children's work in art and design is a potentially problematic area, why should teachers strive to assess their pupils' learning in this area? Essentially, for the following reasons:

- to identify what children have previously learned;
- to identify children's immediate needs;
- to inform children about their progress;
- to inform future planning;
- to inform others of children's progress.

To develop this rationale for assessment, it is helpful to consider a specific example. Assume that you are a Year 3 teacher, taking on a new class, and that the focus for your art and design teaching in the first term is colour and painting.

Box 6.1 Why do we assess children's learning in art and design?

To identify what children have previously learned

Children can predict which two primary colours will make each secondary colour.

Children can change the tone of a colour by adding white paint.

To identify children's immediate needs

Children need to experiment with mixing three primary colours to make a range of tertiary colours, e.g. those relating to autumnal colours.

Children need to experiment with mixing tones in a more controlled way, e.g. by matching to a particular tone.

Children need to experiment with applying paint to paper using a wider range of techniques, e.g. stippling, watering down, etc.

To inform children about their progress

'You're looking carefully at the way the colour is changing as you add more blue and you're making sure that you're using a range of different tones of one colour.'

'You've looked at the textures of the bark that you're painting and you've used brushstrokes that try to represent those textures.'

To inform future planning

Children would benefit from understanding more about how complementary colours can be mixed together (e.g. adding a little red to a bright green will make it a 'leafier' green).

Children need to see examples of how artists have applied paint in a range of ways to create different textures and effects.

To inform others of children's progress

This would take the form of an end-of-year report for parents, or notes to pass on to the subsequent class teacher.

Assessment at the Foundation Stage

The Early Learning Goals identify some key areas in which children's progress can be measured. The Curriculum Guidance for the Foundation Stage recommends that young children should explore colour, texture, shape, form and space that they should use their imagination and should respond in a variety of ways to what they see, hear, smell, touch and feel. Children should, it advises, express and communicate their ideas, thoughts and feelings using a wide range of materials and tools to design and make objects (QCA 2000).

While children at this stage may not require detailed feedback in the way that older pupils might, it is still important for staff in Foundation Stage settings to provide feedback that indicates to children that people value the work that they make sufficiently to comment upon it and to suggest ways in which it might be developed. Many of the teachers that provide effective feedback to young children are those who are keenly aware of some of the ways in which a work might be extended in a way that both builds upon its existing strengths and emphasises its distinctiveness from other children's work. In other words, teachers should strive to communicate to children that a criterion for a successful piece of creative work should not be that it looks just as good as everyone else's in the class.

One problematic aspect of assessing art and design at the Foundation Stage is that young children are generally less concerned than older children with producing a finished 'product'. After working on a painting for ten minutes, a child may have produced a colourful, exuberant masterpiece; five minutes later, still engaged with the process but now working with colours muddied thorough mixing, the vibrancy of the picture has become obscured with impatient grey brushstrokes. Early years practitioners are divided as to whether it is appropriate to 'step in' at a certain point and ask the child if the work is now complete. Surely that would only curtail the child's creative impulse? Yet permitting the child to continue might result in the evidence of the child's developing ability to handle materials and express herself confidently to be obliterated. 'Is it finished?' is a question that troubles artists of all ages!

Forms of assessment at Key Stages 1 and 2

Assessment of children's learning in art and design takes place at different times, in a range of ways and with varying degrees of formality and each form of assessment serves a different purpose. One key area for teachers to reflect upon is the issue of the audience for each form of assessment. Is it an individual pupil or a whole class? A pupil's parents? Their future teachers or other professionals? Maintaining a clear idea of who will benefit from receiving information on pupils' progress should help teachers to focus on what really needs to be communicated. Closely intertwined with each of these aims is the need for teachers to evaluate their own effectiveness: the key question to ask in this respect is, 'If I were to teach this lesson again, what would I change?'

Diagnostic, formative and summative assessments

The statements in Box 6.1 could be categorized either as diagnostic, formative or summative assessments. Diagnostic assessment – identifying what children have previously learned; identifying children's immediate needs – involves working out what learning pupils have achieved as a result of their experiences so far. Formative assessment involves informing children about the progress they are currently making and the ways in which they can reach the targets that they have been set; it will also influence the content of subsequent sessions. The process of formative assessment may take place over a long period of time or within a very short space of time – a teacher might, midway through a lesson, recognize that there are certain misunderstandings among pupils, or that particular techniques need revisiting and revising. Finally, summative assessment evaluates pupils' achievements, and generally involves communicating information about this achievement to parents or other teachers.

Formal assessment

Teachers will also be aware that there are various methods of making assessments of pupils' learning and that these methods can be both formal and informal. An 11-year-old sitting a national test in literacy will be undergoing a formal test; it will be clear that this method of testing would be inappropriate for testing in art and design (even at 16, coursework plays a stronger role in the assessment of pupils' ability in art and design than examinations). Nonetheless, primary teachers are expected to formally assess pupils at the end of each Key Stage against the National Curriculum end of Key Stage Statements, while early years practitioners will use the Curriculum Guidance for the Foundation Stage (CGFS) to assess the pupils' creative development.

Box 6.2 Formal assessment

What counts as evidence?
1 Teacher observations and notes and discussions between child and teacher (or child and child or teacher and teacher);
2 Preparatory work: sketches, etc.;
3 Outcomes: the work itself;
4 Written evidence/child's own view/sketchbooks/portfolios.

Gathering evidence
1 Identify a focus for assessment e.g. look at how children select and use materials, how closely they observe an object when drawing it, how effectively they work as part of a group.
2 Choose a small number of children to observe at any one time: this helps to ensure a higher quality of teacher–child interaction.
3 Try to vary the nature of the assessments taking place; observe children in different contexts on a continual basis, e.g. when engaged in a specific task set by the teacher, or when experimenting in a more individual and personal context.

Box 6.3 Art And Design Assessment Sheet

At the end of each project, during discussion with the teacher, pupils' performance may be recorded on an individual assessment card. These cards enable a record of achievement to be kept throughout the year and to be passed on to each class teacher with whom the pupil may work. These records are available to parents for discussion if necessary.

Name: _____   *Class:* _____   *Teacher:* _____

Project _____

Date _____

Assessment criteria

Preparation and organization   ☐

Observation   ☐

Understanding   ☐

Accuracy   ☐

Cooperation   ☐

Perseverance   ☐

Enjoyment   ☐

Progress   ☐

Assessment is recorded as 1, 2, 3 or 4:
1 = Excellent   2 = Good   3 = Satisfactory   4 = Unsatisfactory

Preparation and organization – Do you settle down quickly at the beginning of the lesson? Do you collect materials and equipment and organize yourself for the task in hand? Do you tidy up your work and put the materials and equipment away?

Observation – Do you look closely at the objects/subject that you are going to draw/paint?

Understanding – Do you plan or draft your ideas out in your sketchbooks? Do you experiment and can you explain your ideas to others?

Accuracy – Do you handle the equipment and art materials correctly? Are you careful and thoughtful about what you are doing when you make art?

Cooperation – Have you cooperated with your peers and teacher by: listening to each other, sharing the equipment and materials, sharing ideas, celebrating each other's achievements?

Perseverance – Have you tried to do the best that you can?

Enjoyment – Have you enjoyed this project? Are you able to explain your reasons?

Progress – Do you feel that you have made some progress in any of the assessment areas?

(Assessment sheet devised by Caroline Corker)

Informal assessment

Many teachers are likely to find that opportunities to provide formal assessments of children's work in art and design may be limited to a few lines written on an end-of-year report. Although when the issue of assessment is raised it is often formal assessment that is discussed, it is arguable that the vast majority of assessments that teachers make of pupils' progress is informal in nature. Indeed, it is partly because of the huge number of responses that teachers make in the classroom that the quality of those responses is sometimes inconsistent or insufficiently challenging or motivating for children. Pressures of time and the demands of the classroom can easily result in superficial responses: 'Lovely! What is it?' Most teachers are aware that they should be saying something more thoughtful, insightful and constructive, but often lack the confidence to respond in the way that children need in order to make progress with their work. These responses, whether they are made to individuals or to the whole class, can be crucial to children's development in art and design.

Children make progress when teachers talk to them about their work; when they are prompted to reflect on what they have achieved with a piece and what might be done to improve it. Children expect to receive praise for their artwork. A child who brings her work to their teacher may be content with a supportive response: 'Lovely, well done. I like the colours you've used.' However, what she would like to hear and what she *needs* to hear may not be the same thing. A child who receives frequent praise and few indications of ways of improving their work is likely to produce work that is repetitive and, ultimately, uninteresting: 'My teacher liked the drawing I did yesterday, and the day before, so I'll do another one the same today.' Children can be encouraged to engage in thoughtful dialogue about their work in art and design if teachers balance the praise they bestow upon their pupils' work with practical suggestions for ways in which it might be developed. By balancing positive comments with constructive interaction, teachers can encourage children to evaluate their work more reflectively and to demonstrate that they are making progress in art and design.

Providing feedback

One key feature of the Literacy and Numeracy hours was the emphasis placed on the importance of providing a plenary session at the end of each lesson, in which pupils have an opportunity to review the learning that has taken place and to sequence it within the context of their continuing development. Teachers may find that this is a useful model upon which to base a strategy for providing feedback during lessons in art and design.

In the course of teaching the class, make a mental note of examples of pupils' work that could serve to illustrate and emphasize the key teaching points of the lesson. While pupils are clearing away at the end of a session, gather together a few examples you want to discuss. Once the whole class has reconvened, show the work – either individually or as a group – and ask for the children's opinions of classmates' efforts. Allow at least a few minutes for this – it takes time for children to absorb what they can see, to formulate responses and to listen to each other's observations. Prompt children to reflect on how well they feel they have realized their intentions for their work. Have they achieved what they set out to do? If not, how might they do this next time? This individualizes assessment and recognizes and values different kinds of work and forms of representation.

You could begin a plenary session by choosing one example of work completed during the lesson and asking the child responsible for it an open question ('Tell us about your painting', perhaps, rather than 'What is it?'). Ask children what they set out to achieve with their paintings and to identify what they think is interesting or successful about the picture and to explain why. Aim to engage children in a dialogue about their work; when making suggestions, bear in mind that the ways in which advice is offered to children can affect their ability to respond to it. Try to begin by accentuating the positive, using praise that targets specific features of the painting: 'I can see that you've really worked hard at blending the tones in your drawing...' before moving on to identify possible areas for development: 'You might think about looking more carefully at ...'

Teachers are required to tread something of a fine line here, since one of the things that is valued about art and design is that there is no 'right' or 'wrong' – that all decisions, for better or for worse, are ultimately made by the artist. Quite often, however, children are not fully aware of exactly what it is that they have done that makes a piece of work successful. Furthermore, we should not forget that children are in school to learn, and if we are aware of one or two ways in which a work of art could possibly be improved, it is our responsibility to share these ideas with pupils. Though be prepared to respond with good grace when your suggestions are ignored!

Box 6.4 Example of a project using ICT

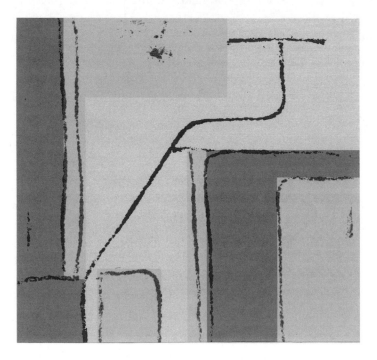

Figure 6.1 ICT print based on detail of map of the London Undeground

The initial composition was created using the drawing and painting tools of an art software package, using a fragment of a map of the London Underground as a starting point.

1 When using computers to make images there is often a temptation to use too many colours and tools. This print is effective partly because it uses a limited range of options.
2 Experiment with extending the print by selecting a section, then copying and pasting it several times into a new document, then reflecting or rotating the selection to create a continuous pattern.

Box 6.5 Example of a drawing project (1)

Figure 6.2 'Picasso-style' collage of features drawn from observation

The features of this Picasso-inspired portrait have been drawn individually and from close observation in pencil, chalk and charcoal before being combined together into a collage.

1 Marks, tones and textures: charcoal has been applied solidly in some places (using the end of the stick), and smudged in others (using the side).
2 Detail: the details of the different features have been closely observed, e.g. the light reflecting in the iris of the eye.
3 Composition: different compositions were explored: pieces were placed in different combinations before being pasted down; additional pieces of paper were added to balance the composition.
4 The work could be developed by experimenting with collections of found textures and integrating them into further portraits.

Box 6.6 Example of a drawing project (2)

Figure 6.3 Figure composition based on individual observational drawings

The aim of this drawing was to combine a collection of drawn figures together in such a way as to create a composition with a feeling of space. Individual drawings were made before being 'redrafted' into one piece.

1   The figure at the bottom of the page has been allowed to 'drop off' the bottom of the page. This gives us the sense of him being much closer to us.
2   Although there is no background to the drawing, each of the figures has been drawn a different size from the others; this creates a strong sense of space.
3   The way in which many of the individual figures have been drawn gives them a real sense of movement.
4   The feelings of space and movement in the drawing could be even stronger if there was a greater variety of line used – thick, strong lines mean that shapes will come forward on the page – thin lines help shapes to recede into the distance.

Summary

The process of looking at children's work, reflecting upon it, of sharing your views and listening to children's own opinions is one that is potentially so informative and fascinating that it should not be missed by any teacher. Informative because, through their artwork, children can reveal aspects of their learning that had been hitherto overlooked or underestimated; fascinating because no two individuals perceive or represent their experiences of the world in quite the same way: art is one area of the curriculum that offers opportunities for *children* to teach *us!*

Bibliography

DfEE/QCA (1999), *The National Curriculum: Handbook for Primary Teachers in England – Key Stages 1 and 2*. London: QCA.

QCA/DfEE (2000), *Curriculum Guidance for the Foundation Stage*. London: QCA/DfEE.

7 Using Artists' Work

Whether visiting a gallery or creating practical work in the classroom, engaging with artists' work offers children valuable opportunities to explore a range of creative ideas, concepts and techniques. But using art to inspire children can be problematic: how can teachers ensure that they make effective use of artists' work in the classroom? And how might the experience of looking at artists' work impact upon children's growing understanding of art and design?

A recurring theme of this chapter is the idea that artists' work could potentially be essential to the art and design curriculum in much the same way that writers' work is essential to the literacy curriculum. The principle that children should read works by a range of authors and that their reading should inform the development of their writing is one that is firmly entrenched in the teaching of literacy. However, evidence suggests that while artists' work is a feature of many of the art lessons taught to children aged 3–11, its role is comparatively peripheral, and that teachers select works of art made by a relatively narrow range of artists (Downing 2005).

There is one important difference between the books children read and the art that children encounter. While there is a long tradition of authors writing for children, it is arguable whether or not artists consider the tastes and needs of children when they are creating their work. Artists may make art for many different and complex reasons – to record, to communicate, to celebrate, to investigate – but rarely, if ever, in order to entertain a class of nine-year-olds visiting an art gallery. Essentially, we are asking children to engage with work that is directed at people much older than they are. We wouldn't expect Year 2 children to tackle a novel by Dickens – so how should we expect them to respond to a sculpture by Henry Moore? Why should artists' work be an important feature of the art and design curriculum? The intention of this chapter is to explore some answers to this question. Its aims are:

1 to provide a rationale for the use of artists' work in primary schools and Foundation Stage settings;

2 to identify and address some of the challenges teachers may face when using artists' work in the classroom;

3 to explore some strategies for developing children's awareness, understanding and appreciation of artists' work.

Why use artists' work?

Since the introduction of the National Curriculum for Art and Design in 1992, primary teachers have been expected to develop children's *knowledge and understanding* of art and design as well as their practical abilities in *designing and making*. The 1992 guidelines stated that children were required to study the works of artists and designers from a range of cultures, with the expectation that these experiences would impact upon the practical work they subsequently produced. Effectively, children were expected to be educated *in* as well as *through* art: as well as learning about a range of practical processes and skills they should also learn about artists and works of art.

In 1999 the two attainment targets for art and design – *Knowledge and Understanding* and *Investigating and Making* – were merged into one, and level descriptors were introduced in order to support teachers making judgements about pupil progress. The new guidelines proposed that children 'should be taught about the roles and purposes of artists, craftspeople and designers working in different times and cultures' and to 'investigate art, craft and design in . . . a variety of genres, styles and cultures' (DfEE 1999, pp. 118–21). Throughout the level descriptors there are references to the need to develop children's responses to works of art:

'They describe what they think or feel about their own and others' work' (Level 1)

'They comment on similarities and differences between their own and others' work' (Level 3)

'They analyse and comment on ideas, methods and approaches used in their own and others' work' (Level 5) (DfEE 1999, p. 33)

The guidelines do not specify that children should study particular artists or designers, but they do strongly suggest that analysing and responding to works of art is an integral part of the curriculum. There is, however, some ambiguity in the language used in the level descriptors: do the references to responding to 'others' work' mean that children should make considered appraisals of work made by established artists – or simply that they should, when required, comment on the work produced by their classmates? Arguably, experience of responding to artists' work could inform children's responses to each other's work. In much the same way that authors' work can inform children's approaches to their own writing, artists' work can inspire children's own practical work in art and design.

Artists' work should arguably play a role in the education of all pupils, however young. The philosophy that underpins much early years education places the child, rather than the curriculum, at the centre of the educational experience. Research into children's attitudes towards making art (Watts 2005) reveals that even young children are able to reflect on the reasons artists may have for creating work. One child interviewed thought that we make art primarily in order 'to communicate with people who don't speak the same language'. Young children are constantly engaged with the challenge of making themselves understood through language. Through encountering artists' work they may realize that there are other forms of communication open to them, forms that place fewer demands on their acquisition of language. The problem of not knowing the word for paintbrush is less of a problem when you are busy using it to make paintings.

The key reasons for using artists' work in schools are:

1   to develop children's awareness, understanding and appreciation of the value of work made by artists, craftspeople and designers from a range of traditions and cultures.
2   to allow children to identify and explore connections between their own practical work and that of artists, craftspeople and designers.
3   to support children as they develop and apply their own critical skills to looking at works of art.

To develop children's awareness, understanding and appreciation of the value of work made by artists, craftspeople and designers from a range of traditions and cultures

Studying a range of artists' work can alert children to the fact that people have made works of art over a period of hundreds, even thousands, of years, and that art and artefacts can provide us with valuable evidence of the past. Crucially, they may begin to understand that art changes over time, that it reflects the society in which it is produced and that through looking closely at works of art we can make informed deductions about changes within societies, people and places.

Children will also develop their awareness that art is made across a range of cultures and that each of these cultures has its own particular styles and traditions. They should become aware that these traditions are handed down through generations and that they are built upon by each subsequent generation. They may also begin to understand that the features of one tradition may influence the development of another. Furthermore, as children develop their awareness of work by contemporary artists, they will appreciate that artists continue to contribute towards the cultures in which they work, and that the work an artist makes is itself part of a tradition that is constantly evolving.

While children will already be aware that a range of processes can be used to make art, studying works by a range of artists will alert them to ways of making and presenting art that will be unfamiliar to them. Some processes used by artists may initially appear to be quite different from those they use in the classroom, yet they may be essentially similar in nature: for example, children may be interested to learn that the process of making a woodcut print has much in common with making a potato print.

Studying artists' work can also develop children's awareness that making art is more complex than simply being able to draw realistically. When children are young they aspire to produce representations of their world that are recognizable to others, and there is a tendency to use art as a form of direct communication: this is me, this is where I live. Young children are often inclined to measure their progress in art by the extent to which they are able to draw accurately. As they grow older, they become aware that while many works of art are representational in this particular way, others are not: they may simply be compositions of lines, colours and shapes. Discovering that making abstract art is a legitimate use of time can be liberating to some children.

Sooner or later, children may come to realize that works of art are *important*. They realize that works of art are held in high esteem by adults and the fact that they are sometimes sold for large amounts of money is evidence to them that someone somewhere is taking them very seriously! More than this, though, the ways in which works of art are presented in the context of the museum or gallery indicates to children that these are objects that may be worthy of some serious reflection.

To allow children to identify and explore connections between their own practical work and that of artists, craftspeople and designers

Although there has been much debate about the relative importance of the two strands of knowledge and understanding and investigating and making within the art and design curriculum, it is arguable that the strands are so closely intertwined as to become interdependent or even indistinguishable. A child who shows an interest in designing or making will, almost inevitably, become interested in developing his/her knowledge and understanding of broader areas of art and design. It is not difficult to provide proof of this: many teachers reading this will, for example, be able to identify a child (often a boy) who demonstrates a passion for drawing through copying images of comic characters. While it is tempting to discourage children from copying, it is arguable that the source of inspiration should not be our key concern – what is important is that the child is is sufficiently enthused by what he/she sees in other people's work to want to make a response to it.

Similarly, children recognize that some of the materials that artists, craftspeople and designers use in their work – pencils, paint, clay – are similar or identical to those that they use in school and at home. They also begin to appreciate that artists use a range of experimental approaches to manipulate these materials in ways that suit their aims. For example, paint is sometimes used in complex ways to construct accurate representations of the visual world, while at other times it is used directly and spontaneously to create compositions and patterns that, while alluding to the visual world, do not seek to represent it 'realistically'. An obvious example, and one expanded upon later in this chapter, would be the paintings made by Jackson Pollock: even young children are able to visualize the methods he used to create his paintings. And as they develop their understanding of the range of processes employed by artists, they are more tempted to experiment themselves: 'I think I understand how this painting was made – now, can I have a go?'!

Studying several examples of work made by a particular artist can help children to understand that each artist develops an individual style over a period of time, a way of making paintings, drawings or sculptures that is unique to them. This is an important part of learning to appreciate one of the central qualities of art and design: artists do not follow a prescriptive set of guidelines that inform them how to make art. One simple measure of the quality of an art and design activity carried out in the classroom is to reflect upon the breadth of the range of outcomes produced by the children. Are many of the pieces of work easily identifiable as being created by particular children? Or do many of the pieces look similar to one another? Children should become aware that they themselves are each developing personal styles of working, in much the same way that artists do.

To support children as they develop and apply their own critical skills to looking at works of art

Evidence suggests that children grow less interested in art and design as they grow older. By the age of 11, many consider that they lack the necessary technical skills to succeed in art and design and conclude that making art is best left to those who demonstrate technical proficiency (Watts 2005). However, the fact that some children lack specific skills should not discourage them from maintaining and developing their interest in art and design. Again, there is a clear connection here with the teaching of literacy: while we expect that few children will become writers, we want each of them to develop and maintain an interest in reading.

Children's critical skills may be sharpened in the gallery or classroom by studying artists' work or by responding to each other's work. It should be emphasized to them that the use of the term *critical* should not imply negative responses; children are likely to associate criticism with being told that they've done something wrong! They should be aware that criticism can and should be constructive in nature. Strategies for encouraging children to develop their critical skills are explored in the section below.

When it comes to responding to artists' work, most children will need little encouragement to express their preferences. Often, however, these preferences may be based on snap judgements about a piece of work; judgements made with little or no reflection. One of the challenges of visiting a museum or gallery is the sheer quantity of work that is on display. It is impossible for an adult – let alone a child – to pay full attention to every work of art in a gallery. Therefore, it is important that teachers structure a gallery visit in a way that allows children to concentrate on a relatively small selection of pieces. Time spent engaging with a single work of art will provide opportunities for children to formulate and justify their opinions, to listen to the opinions of others and to review their first impressions of the piece.

The process of sustained looking encourages us to interrogate the unfamiliar. Children need to be encouraged to appreciate that investing time in a work of art is worthwhile and that, given time, an image or object has the potential to stimulate us, to challenge us and to enrich our lives. A work of art might be glimpsed in a second or gazed at for an hour; it might demand our attention or it may be easily missed. We might notice a detail that had previously been overlooked; we might make a connection between the work we are looking at and other works we have seen in the past. In one sense, the work appears to change before our eyes the longer we look at it – though what is actually happening, of course, is that our *concept* of the work is changing.

Using artists' work: challenges for teachers

While the 1999 National Curriculum guidelines set out the requirement that pupils should 'investigate art, craft and design in . . . a variety of genres, styles and cultures' (DfEE 1999, p. 121), it included none of the specific references to the work of artists and designers that had featured in earlier versions. This was partly in response to evidence of a problem that had emerged over previous years: many teachers, it was suggested, were encouraging their pupils to make artworks that were often little more than copies of the original works or 'unproblematic pastiches of style' (Swift and Steers 1999, p. 10). There was a narrow focus on the exemplar artists referenced in the curriculum orders, artists that tended to be male, white, Western and dead.

The QCA scheme of work for art and design (2000), widely adopted by UK schools, makes brief references to various artists – some familiar, some unfamiliar (and some rather obscure). While these references might be sufficient to encourage some teachers to search for specific images to use in the classroom, references in the scheme to specific works are somewhat cursory and arguably do little to encourage most teachers to hunt down examples of their work.

Responding to art: discussion

Whether in the gallery or the classroom, simply introducing children to works of art is no guarantee that the experience will in any way be memorable or beneficial for them. Stepping inside a gallery, they might be overwhelmed by a dozen paintings, each demanding their attention; without some support and guidance it is likely that none will leave more than a fleeting impression upon them. There is an argument that a painting or sculpture should not require additional information aimed at informing or appealing to a particular audience, that a work of art should *speak for itself*. But anyone who has taught any group of children for any length of time will be all too aware that the fact that someone is speaking is no guarantee that anyone is listening! Children need to be led gently towards a work of art, they need to be encouraged to ask questions about it and they need to be provided with strategies for unravelling its mysteries. So what is the teacher's role in this process? And what responses are we seeking from children?

As well as providing a source of inspiration for children's practical work in art and design – some ideas for which are explored in the next section – studying artists' work offers children opportunities to develop a range of skills relating to looking, thinking, listening and responding. The teacher's role in supporting the development of these skills involves:

1 selecting examples of artists' work for children to investigate;
2 introducing the work – first impressions;
3 encouraging close observation – looking at detail;
4 managing discussion about the work.

Selecting artists' work to investigate

A work of art could be selected for use in the classroom for one of several reasons. We might select a work of art that relates closely to learning in another curriculum area. A nineteenth century family portrait, for example, could be used as primary evidence for children researching the Victorian era, while representations of religious icons can form a strong visual focus to RE lessons (using the 'image' function of a search engine can quickly produce results that can then be displayed on an interactive whiteboard). Teachers should be aware, however, that while the practice of using works of art as sources of information about other times and cultures is valuable, it should be emphasized to children that the value of art extends far beyond a means of providing evidence about the past. One advantage that teachers of children aged 3–11 have over their colleagues in secondary schools is the opportunities that arise for cross-curricular teaching: the use of artists' work need not be restricted to art lessons, but could permeate all curriculum areas.

In selecting a work of art for use in the classroom, teachers should be aware of the opportunities it will offer children to gain a deeper understanding of specific aspects of art and design. A work of art might be selected for use in the classroom because of its content: the scene it portrays or the story it tells; it might be chosen for its atmospheric evocation of particular mood; or it might be chosen to prompt children's responses to the ways in which the artist has used a technique or particular materials. A work of art might be studied for its own sake – responses to the work will come in the form of discussion – or it might be studied because of its potential to inspire children to make their own practical work.

Alternatively, we may choose a particular work because it is one that we as teachers are particularly interested in and enthusiastic about. Children are quick to recognize and respond to genuine enthusiasm: teachers will be familiar with the way in which a few inspired readings of a particular book can quickly help it to become a class favourite, and similar levels of enthusiasm can be inspired by a work of art.

Perhaps the most interesting reason for selecting a particular work is *curiosity*. We may choose a particular work to share with children not because we *know* why it appeals to us but because we want to *find out* why it appeals to us. We may want the opportunity to hear the opinions of others, in the hope of understanding more clearly what it is about the work that intrigues us. Through introducing the work to the class and through listening to children's thoughts and opinions, our perceptions of the work are likely to be clarified, to be reinforced or even to change altogether.

Introducing the work

Children respond warmly to the notion that encountering a work of art is not unlike meeting a person for the first time. We can see immediately how someone looks – but it takes us some time to find out about that person, to get to know them, to understand what it is about them that makes them unique, that makes them special.

But introducing a work of art to children can be problematic. While children may be curious about the work and some may be ready to make observations about it, they might also suspect that there is a set of 'right' responses that their teacher is seeking from them. Rather than investing time in reflecting upon the qualities of an image or object, they may look to the teacher to prompt them towards a specific reading of the work. Encourage children to make a note of their first impressions of an artwork – even if it is only one word – because as soon as they begin to listen to others' observations and opinions, those first impressions can be difficult to retrieve.

From the beginning, introduce children to the idea that the experiences we bring to a work of art will affect the way we perceive it. Essentially, the question is: Are we all looking at the same picture? Children will initially be inclined to answer 'yes'; but, as soon as observations and opinions are exchanged, they will be surprised to discover how people can perceive a work of art in different ways.

Teachers are trained to encourage children to ask questions, and are encouraged to reflect on the nature of those questions: are they open questions that can be answered in many ways, or closed questions that require one specific answer? Initially, children are likely to ask closed questions about artworks. They will need some time to confirm for themselves exactly what it is that they are looking at before beginning to formulate their own opinions and ideas about it. Some will want to know how the work has been made: is it a drawing, painting or photograph? They may want to know who made the work, where they were and when they lived. Once children are satisfied that their initial questions have been answered, they will be better prepared to move beyond learning facts about a work of art towards studying it in greater depth.

Looking at detail

Once these facts about a work have been shared, teachers should encourage children to examine the detail of the work:

1 What can you see?
2 What do you think is happening?
3 How is the person in the painting feeling?
4 What makes you think he looks sad?
5 Describe the colours that the artist has used in the painting.

If children find it difficult to focus their attention on the detail of a work, challenge them to play a game in which they take it in turns to describe a detail of the work that has not been noticed by anyone else: the child who has the last word wins!

Then aim to challenge the children by asking them questions of a higher order – questions that are both thoughtful and thought-provoking, and that challenge them to look closely at the work and to justify their responses:

1 How do the colours of the painting affect its mood?
2 What evidence is there that this picture was painted many years ago?
3 What do you think happened immediately before the scene that we can see? What do you think might happen next?
4 If the people in the picture could talk, what might they say?

This approach links closely with the model proposed by Rod Taylor. Taylor (1992) recommends that the steps children take towards engaging with artists' work should be clearly structured by the teacher. He suggests that children should first establish the *content* of a work of art, before analysing its *form* – the shapes that combine to make its composition, the *process* that has been used to create the work and the *mood* that it subsequently communicates to the viewer:

> (The content/form/process/mood model) has the potential to encourage and stimulate pupils to conjecture before works of art in relevant and imaginative ways. It can aid them in the process of valuing and clarifying their own responses, opinions and judgements arrived at through the posing of a whole range of basic questions prompted by each of the four areas in turn.
>
> (Taylor 1992, p. 70)

Taylor identifies a range of educational implications of the model, including the suggestion that 'it provides an invaluable analytical tool for pupils to engage with art works of which they have no prior knowledge, enabling them to study them at more objective levels and to bring direct responses to bear' (ibid. p. 86). Teachers may choose to emphasize to children this structure for framing responses to works of art by providing worksheets that explicitly encourage them to address each of these categories in turn. Making brief written responses to a work can crystallize children's thoughts and develop their confidence in communicating their opinions.

Managing discussion

While Taylor's model is a useful way of guiding children towards analysing works of art, it is arguable that many artists would prefer their works to be a stimulus for creative thought in their viewers. By making a work of art and displaying it in a studio or gallery or publishing it in a book or on a website, an artist is presenting us with the first line of a conversation, a conversation that now relies upon us, the viewers, to continue. Teachers should strongly consider the advantages of introducing a structured approach to developing classroom discussions that, while initiated by works of art, may develop to encompass a range of themes that children perceive as being related to the work.

Fisher (1998) proposes the establishment of a *community of enquiry* in the classroom through developing a 'Thinking Circle', providing a structure for classroom discussion that challenges children to think, share, express and revise their thoughts and beliefs. Many teachers will be familiar with the concept of Circle Time as a means of facilitating thoughtful exchanges within the classroom, and although the Thinking Circle may resemble Circle Time in some respects, it is more structured and concentrated, and one essential difference is that it requires the provision of a specific stimulus that should focus the discussion.

Having presented a stimulus for discussion, the teacher lists questions about the stimulus offered by participants of the discussion before managing the process of selecting one of the questions for an extended discussion. The teacher then aims to manage the discussion in such a way that participants respond directly to *each other* rather than through the teacher. Finally, the discussion is reviewed before further potential lines of enquiry are identified. Fisher suggests that the stimulus for the discussion should ideally be something that has the potential to challenge children's assumptions. It might be a story, a philosophical question (How do we know we're alive? What is a good person?), or even a piece of music. A work of art however is, arguably, an ideal starting point. As affecting as a story or poem may be, it may easily be misheard or misremembered. A key advantage of using an artwork to stimulate discussion is that during the discussion children can *continue to look* at the artwork, to reflect on it and to review their opinions of it in the light of hearing those expressed by other members of the class.

An example to explore

Figure 7.1 Photograph – Mark Crick

Opposite are two sets of questions prompted by this photograph, divided into two categories: 'Factual' questions and 'Thinking' questions. These two categories are roughly equivalent to 'closed' and 'open' questions: a closed question has only one correct answer, whereas an open question can be answered in many different ways. By considering the theme of a factual question, children may be able to rephrase it in ways that will make it a more thought-provoking question, one that might stimulate a reflective discussion. Initially, the questions that children will ask about a work of art are likely to be factual in nature. However, the more experience they have of generating questions, selecting questions for discussion and engaging in discussions prompted by these questions, the more quickly they will be able to recognize that some questions offer more potential for discussion than others.

Box 7.1 Developing 'thinking questions'

'Factual'/'closed' questions	Theme	'Thinking'/'open' questions
How old are these people?	Age	Do we change as we get older? Or do we remain the same person? Is it better to be old or young?
What game are they playing?	Games	Why do people play games? Is it important to win when you play a game? Do adults play games for the same reasons as children?
Are these people rich or poor?	Wealth and poverty	Are rich people happier than poor people? Would you be happier if you were rich?
Who took the picture?	Identity	Why was the photograph taken? Why do people take photographs of each other? How do you feel when you look at photographs of yourself, or of your family?
Why are they all sitting the same way?	Composition	How does the fact that the people are sitting the same way make the picture more interesting?

Further questions might centre on the visual qualities of the picture such as the range of the tones and textures of the materials. An interesting way to conclude a discussion would be to ask children whether they think the artwork has changed during the course of the discussion. Does it look the same, but *feel* different? Did something that someone said make you see the picture in a different way? Has your opinion of the picture changed because of the discussion? Questions such as these offer children opportunities to reflect on their developing understanding of how works of art have the potential to change the ways we think and feel about things. Perhaps not every teacher would consider that an art lesson would be well spent simply looking at and talking about a single picture. Yet curiously, the acts of looking and of making a personal response to that which is seen have strong parallels with that most traditional of art activities, observational drawing. Both demand a sustained period of time to be invested if the experience is to be worthwhile.

Responding to artists' work: practical work

It is a truism about art that everything has already been done, that every idea has been thought of, that there is nothing new to be created. Although this a negative perspective to assume, teachers can choose to take it positively: for almost anything that is being taught, there will, somewhere, be a work of art that can both inspire and enrich the practical activities planned for the classroom. In this section, we will reflect in detail on one practical activity inspired by the work of a particular artist, Jackson Pollock. The activity involves rolling marbles through paint and then on to paper. This activity has been selected because it is one that is essentially simple yet potentially complex; it is one that can be challenging to ten-year-olds yet accessible to three-year-olds; it is one that does not depend on the acquisition of any specific skill, yet it offers opportunities for children to reflect thoughtfully on ways in which it can be developed and extended.

Selecting artists' work

When selecting a work of art to use as inspiration for children's practical work, a key question to ask is: What is it that could make this artist's work interesting, inspiring or challenging to children? In the case of Pollock's work, it is arguably the fact that the paintings seem to be composed solely of random marks, marks that nonetheless combine to create compositions that are balanced and 'complete'. Pollock's paintings encourage us to reflect on issues of *control*: specifically, the extent to which the artist – whether an adult or a child – should expect to assume control over every aspect of the work they produce. The activity also offers opportunities for children to produce work that is abstract – that is to say, art that is non-representational.

Pollock's paintings of the mid-1950s challenged many people's preconceptions about the nature of painting. They were made by dripping thin paint directly onto canvas stretched across the floor to create a complex composition of intersecting lines and splashes. Ever since, abstract paintings such as Pollock's have regularly prompted the remark that 'a child of five could do that'. Intended as an insult, the remark might also be seen as a challenge – especially if you happen to be a child of five!

There are valuable lessons to be learned from studying the work of artist such as Pollock. His method for making paintings challenges the perception of the artist as someone who is in complete control over the work they produce. His work highlights the role that chance can play in the creation of an artwork; it prompts us to value the potential unpredictability of art materials and to appreciate that the unexpected solution can be more valuable than the one that is consciously sought.

Another reason for selecting Pollock's work as a focus is that children are unlikely to attempt (and no one would be capable of making) an exact replica of one of his paintings! Children are sometimes required to copy text from a board or a book; even when they are asked to paraphrase text, some will slavishly copy the source material. The same can be true in art lessons. Informing children that an example of an artist's work is being shown to them 'only as a guideline' and informing them that 'it's not meant to be copied' is fine – assuming, of course, that they are listening. Some (auditory learners, perhaps) will be, but others (visual learners, possibly) will see a teacher pointing at a picture and pointing at their paper and assume that their task is quite straightforward – if rather demanding. (Furthermore, if we recognize the impossibility of copying a painting, we might reflect on the nonchalance with which we might ask children to draw a tree – an equally daunting task.)

Beginning the lesson

You might decide to show children an example of Pollock's work before they begin to make their own paintings; alternatively, you might choose to introduce the work half way through a sequence of lessons, when children have had time to explore ideas without feeling a need to produce work that echoes the artist's. Should you be concerned that seeing the 'originals' might restrict children's investigations into their materials, you might even decide to withhold showing images of the artist's work until they have completed a sequence of activities. A sequence of lessons inspired by Pollock's work could begin with the teacher showing pupils an example of a painting made in a style similar to Pollock's and asking his/her pupils how they *think* the painting has been made.

This example was made by rolling two painted marbles around on a piece of paper inside a cardboard box. The teacher may choose to describe this process while showing the resulting piece. Alternatively, he/she may choose to show pupils the finished piece and ask them how they think it was made. The painting *could* have been made by:

Figure 7.2 Marble rolling

- using straws to blow paint around the paper;
- pouring thin paint directly from the tube on to the paper;
- painting lengths of string and dragging them around the paper;
- covering sticks in paint and scratching the surface of the paper.

Each 'wrong' answer provided by pupils can become a new activity for the children to explore. Several of the suggestions could easily be anticipated by the teacher and resources – straws, string, sticks – could easily be gathered in advance of the lesson for children to explore their ideas. If four groups were each to work on a different activity, the results could then be compared at the end of the lesson, which could provide valuable opportunities for pupils to engage in describing and contrasting their paintings. How does a painting made with marbles look different from one made with string? Or from one made with straws? The resulting dialogue will inevitably lead the children towards discussing the abstract qualities of the work: the nature of the lines, the texture of the paint. In the following lesson, activities could be rotated among the groups, giving children opportunities to build upon each other's ideas.

Making decisions

Rolling painted marbles around on sheet of paper is a simple activity that almost any child can carry out. Yet in the process of making the work, there are a number of decisions that need to be made. To fully appreciate this you will need to make the piece of work yourself. You will need some paper, some paint, some marbles and a box. Even if you are only visualizing this process, how many decisions have you already made? What colour is the paper you chose? What size? Is it rectangular? Does it need to be? Does it fit in the box? Can you find a bigger box? What kind of paint have you chosen? Watercolour? Ready-mixed? How much water will you mix with it? How many marbles will you use? Will they all be the same size? . . . And you haven't even started painting yet.

Once you have begun, the next set of decisions needs to be made: Where will you place the first marble? The second? The third? How will you move the marbles around the paper, with your fingers or by moving the box? Will you watch the marbles and try to control their movements, or will you close the lid of the box and rattle the marbles around? And then the question that every artist asks of each piece: Is it finished? If not, why not? Does the composition feel right? Are some areas too busy, others too empty? Is there too much of one colour and too little of another? Is there a balance of thick marks (made by the marbles when they are loaded with paint) and thin marks (made by the marbles when they are running out of paint)?

If these may seem like relatively trivial decisions, remember that they are much the same as those that occupy 'real' artists when they are making their work. While artists may have a range of complex and personal reasons *why* they make their work, the internal dialogue that takes place during its making is often a process of relatively mundane decisions – left a bit, right a bit, lighter, darker. Each of these decisions, however much you are aware of them at the time, will have some influence on the appearance of your painting. The more decisions teachers make for their pupils, the more likely it is that the resulting work will be dull and repetitive. The more frequently teachers encourage pupils to make such decisions, the less dependent they will be upon influences from work by artists or by other pupils around them and the more varied and interesting their work will be.

Extending the lesson

Experimenting with materials in much the way that Pollock did, with no pressure to create a recognizable image, can be a liberating experience for children. They have the opportunity to discover that, rather than learning to make a work of art in a way tightly prescribed by a teacher, there are many right answers to the problem – a point raised by Eisner:

> The arts teach children that problems can have more than one solution and that questions can have more than one answer. The arts celebrate diversity. While the teacher of spelling is not particularly interested in ingenuity of response from students, the arts teacher seeks it.
>
> (Eisner 2003, p. 17)

The marble-rolling activity could lead on to a range of further activities, each of which allows pupils to experiment with making compositions over which they have only a limited amount of control. Encourage your pupils to reflect on what they plan to change about the activity (and what they plan to keep the same). For example, consider:

1 scale – make larger paintings in the playground by rolling balls through paint;
2 colour and tone – expand or restrict the options available;
3 collaboration – work in pairs, groups or as a whole class;
4 control – move the paper beneath the marbles to create a semi-controlled pattern.

Once children have experimented with marble paintings, offer some or all of the following as further activities in the sequence. These activities will enable some children to move forwards – to learn new processes and develop existing skills – and others to move sideways – to experiment with alternative approaches to making art.

Drawing

Use oil pastels to cover your paper with interlocking shapes; draw a second, darker layer of oil pastel over the top, then use a coin to scrape away random sections of the second layer to reveal the first.

Painting

Throw strips of coloured ribbon down randomly onto paper and make a still life painting of the arrangement (i.e. a figurative picture of something abstract!).

Printmaking

Cover a thick piece of card with a thin layer of PVA glue and randomly twist lengths of string into it; allow the glue to dry then roll ink across the surface and print onto paper.

Textiles

Stretch fabric across a frame, then sew lengths of wool up from beneath the fabric and across the top to create a random cross-hatched pattern of straight lines.

Batik

Use a *tjanting* tool to drip hot wax in random patterns across a stretched piece of fabric; paint over with fabric dye and wait for it to dry before melting the wax using a hot iron and newspaper

Collage

Paint a sheet of paper with random shapes made from a range of tones of one colour; repeat on a second sheet with a different colour, then tear the two paintings into strips and combine to make a new piece.

ICT

Use paintbrush tools to create a random pattern on the screen, then select a rectangular section to copy and paste into a new file; paste this section several times and experiment with rotating and reflecting each layer to make a repeat pattern.

Summary

This chapter has presented a case for the inclusion of artists' work in Foundation Stage and primary education settings, and has proposed that works of art can not only provide inspiration for children's own creative practical work, but also present valuable starting points for reflective discussion. It has been written with the understanding, however, that relatively few teachers of children aged 3–11 currently have the specialist knowledge that will enable them to respond to ideas proposed in this chapter to the extent that they might like, and that all teachers have only limited time to implement new approaches to their practice.

In response to this, it is suggested that the majority of teachers are inclined to underestimate the depth and relevance of their knowledge and understanding of art and design, and that they already possess a specific range of skills which could be applied to using artists' work more widely in their teaching. Specifically, these teachers typically have high levels of expertise in the teaching of literacy. They are aware of a range of strategies for teaching and learning in this area, and it is arguable that many of the strategies they employ to engage children with authors' work could easily be adapted to engaging children with artists' work. The study of authors' work is seen as intrinsically linked with developing children's creative writing, a theme taken up by Buchanan:

> In many respects, the parallels between learning in English and in art and design are striking. The acts of creative writing and making art are both concerned with conveying feeling, meaning and response to the perceived world, using a particular language, with its attendant set of codes, conventions and grammar. Writing and art-making are not simply concerned with the utilitarian skill of construction.

(Buchanan 1995, p. 31)

Teachers want children to develop an understanding, an appreciation and a love of literature; they want children to learn to write not only accurately but also creatively; they want children to demonstrate that they are able to absorb influences from writers who are older, more highly skilled, able to communicate their ideas effectively and to inform and inspire their readers. Consider a child who, while lacking the knowledge or skill to write creatively or even coherently, is nonetheless able to respond thoughtfully to stories or poems written by others. Can this child not accurately be described as one who is succeeding in literacy? Similarly, consider a child who struggles to draw accurately or to paint convincingly, but is able to make intuitive, thoughtful, articulate responses to works of art. Could this child not accurately be described as one who is succeeding in art and design?

Art is, or can be – or even *should* be – a difficult subject to study seriously at any level. It is arguable that the process of engaging with work by artists such as Jackson Pollock can present challenges for many adults, let alone children. And it is true that artists rarely, if ever, make work with the intention that it will appeal to children – so are we being realistic when we hope that they will relate to it or understand it?

Perhaps children should grow to understand that works of art are often mysterious, that they might not reveal everything to us – but that this is part of their appeal, part of the spell they cast over us. We all bring our own experiences to an encounter with a work of art, and the experiences that children bring can be as valid as those of anyone else. Children may not always understand exactly *what* artists intend to communicate through their work, but they will sense that they are saying *something* – and that it might be something worthy of investigation and reflection.

Bibliography

Buchanan, M. (1995), 'Making art and critical literacy: a reciprocal relationship', in R. Prentice (ed.) *Teaching Art and Design*, London: Cassell.

DfEE (1999), *National Curriculum: Handbook for Primary Teachers in England – Key Stages 1 and 2*. London: DfEE.

Downing, D. (2005), 'School art – what's in it?', *International Journal of Art and Design Education*, 24(3): 271.

Eisner, E. (2003), 'What do the arts teach?' *International Journal of Arts Education*, 1(1): 7–17 Taiwan.

Fisher, R. (1998), *Teaching Thinking: Philosophical Enquiry in the Classroom*. London: Cassell.

Hickman, R. (2005), 'A short history of "critical studies" in art and design education', in R. Hickman (ed.), *Critical Studies in Art and Design Education*. Bristol: Intellect.

QCA (2000), *Art and Design Teacher's Guide*. London: QCA.

Swift, J. and Steers, J. (1999), 'A manifesto for art in schools', *Journal of Art and Design Education* 18(1): 7–13.

Taylor, R. (1992), *The Visual Arts in Education: Completing the Circle*. London: Falmer Press.

Watts, R. (2005), 'Attitudes to making art in the primary school', *International Journal of Art and Design Education* 24(3): 243–53.

Photograph on p. 146 used with permission of Mark Crick.

Useful Websites

www.barbican.org.uk
  Barbican Centre

www.thebritishmuseum.ac.uk
  The British Museum

www.designmuseum.org
  The Design Museum

www.hayward.org.uk
  Hayward Gallery

www.ica.org.uk
  Institute of Contemporary Art

www.nationalgallery.org.uk
  The National Gallery

www.npg.org.uk
  National Portrait Gallery

www.photonet.org.uk
  Photographers' Gallery

www.royalacademy.org.uk
  The Royal Academy of Arts

www.saatchi-gallery.co.uk
  Saatchi Gallery

www.serpentinegallery.org
  Serpentine Gallery

www.southlondongallery.org
South London Gallery

www.tate.org.uk
Tate Galleries

www.vam.ac.uk
Victoria and Albert Museum

www.whitechapel.org
Whitechapel Gallery

8

Equal Opportunities

Chapter Outline

All children are entitled to art and design education. In the UK this is a statutory entitlement: teachers are legally obliged to ensure that all children are educated in art and design as part of a broad and balanced National Curriculum. This provision should not only be seen in legal terms however. It is important to understand the educational value of art and design. The discussion of this in earlier chapters provides the justification for enabling all children to participate in it, whatever their abilities, gender, ethnicity, religion, background or age.

In the interests of entitlement, there is a need to address some assumptions that may influence practice and may ordinarily remain unquestioned. For instance, criteria can be used to make judgements about children's ability in art and design that might, unintentionally but unjustifiably, exclude some children. Furthermore, the way art is conceived can determine the kinds of experience children have. There is a need to ensure that this does not curtail the development of children's potential in the area, rather than helping it to flourish. There is a need to be aware of the messages that can inadvertently be given to children by the place it is given in the curriculum, as well as in the kinds of experiences and activities that are provided. In this chapter, these issues are discussed along with issues around gender, ethnicity and cultural diversity and inclusion of children with special educational needs. The need to think about the breadth and quality of the experience given to children in art and design is considered, as well as the need to ensure that no child is disadvantaged in their art education as a result of who they are.

It has already been pointed out that art and design is not always seen to be an essential aspect of every child's learning in the same way as other subject areas. One reason for this is that it is simply not valued as highly. There can be very different attitudes towards art and design than towards other, traditionally more valued areas, such as literacy or numeracy. The curriculum pressures on 'non-core' subjects which have to some extent marginalized art and design were discussed in Chapter 2. Sometimes, however, it can seem to be for the opposite reason – that art and design is seen as an elite subject best reserved for a select few rather than an area of life and learning for everyone. This perception rests on the idea that the only people who can benefit from education in art are those who are talented. Many readers will themselves have experienced some form of discouragement or even discrimination in art and design lessons, on the grounds that they were simply 'no good' at art. The result of this experience can be that people 'drop' art and design at the earliest opportunity, often with a feeling of failure in the subject and a sense that it is not for them. By way of comparison, it is unlikely that a child who was having difficulties in reading would be seen to be lacking the necessary talent and that teaching them to read should therefore be a low priority. On the contrary, they would be given special help to overcome their difficulties. As with any other aspect of children's education, teachers have to ensure that all children, whatever their apparent levels of ability, have access to art and design in the curriculum.

As has already been argued (see Chapter 4), if art is always left until Friday afternoons as a kind of relaxation at the end of a tiring week, then the quality of experience may be compromised. Similarly, if art is only ever included as a means of achieving learning in other areas of the curriculum, then there is less scope for developing the understanding that can only be gained through art and design: children need to be provided with opportunities to acquire the concepts and skills that are specific to learning through art and design, and to learn about the world through the distinctive means that art and design offer. These issues, already raised in other chapters, have a direct bearing on the question of making adequate provision in art and design that is accessible to all children.

Ways of thinking about art and design education: inclusive or exclusive?

Clearly, to be identified as 'no good at art' is potentially damaging in terms of children's life experience, as it can have the effect of putting them off any engagement in art and design activity, not only in the sense of making art themselves, but also in experiencing the work of others. Art and design are communicative practices which enable human beings to develop and question their intellectual and emotional response to their experience. Art and design are arguably essential to any individual's education, especially in the highly visual world of the twenty-first century. Furthermore, to be visually illiterate and to have an impoverished experience of the visual dimension of the world can lead towards an inability to make judgements and choices about it. Often, a very narrow range of criteria is used to identify a child's abilities in art, usually linked to being able to draw, and moreover, to being able to draw in a way that is particularly difficult. The good artist at school is often seen to be the child who can produce an accurate, life-like rendering of some recognizable object. This kind of criterion potentially excludes a large number of children. (For a discussion of a different way of looking at children's drawing, which links it to their learning and thinking, see Cox 2005.)

Crucially, teachers need to be aware of how they might be making judgements of their pupils and their abilities to ensure that they are not, unthinkingly, excluding children on the basis of such narrow criteria. Instead, they need to recognize the wide range of ways in which children might demonstrate artistic ability. Some children may have limited skill in drawing in the conventionally accepted way, but may confidently construct three dimensional models; some may love to arrange and design the role play area while others may communicate their ideas through a strong sense of colour. Some may be particularly sensitive to pattern and texture, perhaps demonstrated through printmaking and collage, while others may embody their ideas through puppet making and performance. All children represent and communicate ideas through manipulating objects and materials in their environment, transforming one thing into another. There is a need to address assumptions that are so easily made about what it is to work in art and design, to ensure that all children benefit from an art and design education, whatever their apparently inherent abilities.

The open-endedness of art and design activity

Given children's needs for education in art and design, there are further questions around how teachers ensure that equal opportunities are provided for all children, both girls and boys, of all abilities, and of all ethnic groups. In art and design, value is placed on individual response and interpretation. 'Rather than there being a "right answer", there are as many answers as there are individuals' (Herne 1995, p. 2). This inherent diversity means that the subject area itself allows every child's ideas, deriving from whatever source within themselves and their social and cultural worlds, to be of equal worth. Teaching in the subject requires that all children's ideas are encouraged and valued and that teaching strategies enable children to explore and develop their own ideas, rather than having their teacher's ideas, or a particular way of making art, imposed upon them. The teacher whose desired end product might be a display of ducks on a pond, and who provides card templates and white paper to make the bodies and orange triangles to stick on for beaks, is neither demonstrating the value of diversity of response nor encouraging individual creativity.

The open-endedness of art and design can seem daunting to some teachers. It can seem that the teacher has no role. If the focus is on the child's own ideas it can appear to be a subject without content to be taught. This is a misinterpretation. There are, indeed, important areas of learning within art and design. It can be useful to see this in two ways. On the one hand, children need to acquire the tools to communicate their own ideas. They need to become aware of the range of strategies through which they can make art, and to develop appropriate abilities. This can be through mastery of skills and techniques in using varied media, and through developing their understanding of the elements of visual and tactile experience so they have a greater range of practical and intellectual resources available to them. On the other hand, children's ideas do not develop in isolation from their experience and developing understanding of what goes on around them. As with any other area of the curriculum, learning takes place in a socio-cultural context. In other words, children make sense of their world by experiencing the way in which others do this in their social and cultural group, and this influences the range of meanings that they bring to any new situation. It is through this interplay of their individual understanding and the conceptualizations within the wider society that children construct their own meanings. Teachers play a central role in mediating this wider world. However, this should open up opportunities for individual interpretation, rather than close them down. The richer the teacher's provision, the wider the scope for children's creativity.

> ## Box 8.1 Opening up opportunities
>
> Teachers need to:
> - offer wide-ranging and interesting visual and tactile experiences, and to encourage close observation, so that children's attention is drawn to the visual richness of their environment.
> - provide the stimuli for children to explore their responses to their experience of the world through visual representations.
> - explore children's responses through interaction and talk.
> - make the whole range of representational options available to children so they can develop their ideas (see Kress 1997).
> - provide experience of the diversity and richness of what other artists have made, to broaden children's understanding of the variety of means that can be used to communicate and the variety of contexts in which art is made. If art and design are communicative practices, then it is the role of the teacher to enable the child to develop this form of language, to become visually literate, to help him/her develop an artistic vocabulary of marks and form and, moreover, to engage with the social and cultural worlds in which it can be given meaning.

This view of the nature of art and design is common to all the chapters in this book, but is reiterated here to show its implications for inclusive practice. Rather than standing back or abandoning their role, teachers must make provision for learning in these ways so that all children can realize their creative potential; in the interests of equal opportunities, what is provided by the teacher must take into account individuals' differing needs. This means that teachers need to be sure that they do not exclude children through expectations of them that they might unconsciously hold. They need to ensure that both girls and boys, all social and ethnic groups – including travellers, refugees and asylum-seekers, and those for whom English is an additional language – and all children with special educational needs are provided for. The principles of inclusion are established in the curriculum from the Foundation Stage: 'No child should be excluded or disadvantaged because of ethnicity, culture or religion, home language, family background, special educational needs, disability, gender or ability' (QCA/DfEE 2000, p. 11).

Gender

How can this be brought about in practice? One area that must be addressed is the kind of media that are made available to children. Children should not be restricted to particular materials on the grounds of their gender, or their ideas unwittingly be influenced by gender stereotyping. For instance, if teachers are to provide equal opportunities, then they need to make sure that they are not giving boys more access to resistant materials and tools, such as wood, and encouraging only girls to do textile work. One only has to look at the gender bias in art schools between departments of fine art and textile departments to see that the influence of such stereotyping still persists. The latter have, over time, been devalued in various ways – for example, textile arts have often been referred to as craft, rather than art, which has resulted in their being regarded as significantly lower in status (see Chapter 3). Such prejudice can and should be challenged by teachers – in the early years of children's education onwards – making sure that they themselves do not favour those forms of art that are traditionally 'male' over those that are traditionally 'female'.

Children may have predilections for certain types of media and ideas, perhaps arising from the gender-biased influences they have already experienced. Again, there might appear to be a contradiction between the aim of encouraging children to pursue their individual directions and the case for introducing them to a full range of possibilities. If they want to work through construction, or digital media, for instance, to the exclusion of anything else, shouldn't they be allowed to follow their own preferences? Doesn't encouraging them to explore alternatives prevent them from developing their own ideas? In reality, if they are *not* encouraged to learn new or different approaches, this in itself limits the scope for them to develop their own ideas. It is through broadening the child's experience and interests that teachers will enrich the child's own work. To provide equal opportunities, it is important to make sure that a balance is struck. It is in the educational interests of the child both to be provided with the widest range of experiences and learning that challenges any stereotypical choices, and also to be given the opportunity to pursue their own directions. The child who is drawn only to working in one medium should be given the opportunity and encouragement to try others.

There is also a need to look critically and carefully at the art and design work made by other artists that is used in the classroom. The artists that come to mind, in the first instance, can tend to be male. Indeed, it can be difficult to recall examples of female artists' work, especially from historical contexts. In the contemporary art scene in Britain, there are some high profile and controversial women, such as Tracey Emin and Rachel Whiteread, as well as established figures such as Gillian Ayers, Elizabeth Blackadder and Sonia Boyce, but these well-known women represent only a fraction of the number of women art and design practitioners. In earlier periods of history, women were working as artists but were suppressed in the context of male-dominated, patriarchal societies. This occurred not only during their lifetimes but was subsequently sustained by the male orientation of the dominant art discourse and art history and through the curators of museums and galleries. Art historians such as Parker and Pollock (1981) investigated and analysed this gender imbalance, bringing to light the work of 'hidden' women artists and 'The Women Artists' Slide Library' also campaigned for the recognition of women from the 1970s onwards. (It closed in 2002 but is now part of University of London Goldsmiths' College Women's Art Library.) There are now popular publications that provide comprehensive information on the range of female artists (see, for example, Sterling 1995). It is most important that teachers represent the work of women as well as men in their classrooms to give positive messages to girls that art and design are practices which are fully open to them.

Cultural diversity

Turning to the issues around inclusion in relation to ethnicity, the same arguments apply. If equal opportunities are to be provided for children from all ethnic groups then it is essential to value the forms of art that reflect the cultural backgrounds of the children in the class, school or local community and make sure that these are represented.

Box 8.2 Key considerations

- Teachers should include art and design practices that relate to the cultural contexts of their pupils: for example, teachers who are sensitive to the Rajasthani backgrounds of some children in their class may introduce appropriate methods of paper making or tie-dying.

- Teachers must take account of the cultural mores of the children they teach; there is, for example, some confusion around the issue of representation of the human form for Muslim children. Many teachers are under the misapprehension that Muslim children cannot make figurative art, but in fact, this is only the case in relation to religious iconography. They can join in fully with all kinds of art making, including figurative art, which is found in a variety of forms in secular Islamic art. They can also study Western traditions of religious art as well as those of Islam. However, if children are making their own responses to religious art, then Muslim children would draw on their cultural traditions of pattern and calligraphy rather than iconic figuration. (See Herne 1995.)

It is important that children who speak English as an additional language are not disadvantaged by the art curriculum and that they are not seen as having learning difficulties. For children learning English, art offers a particular avenue for inclusion, in that they may find there is more scope for communication through visual means than by using verbal language.

There are further issues around equal opportunities in the context of ethnicity that go beyond making specific provision for children from black and Asian communities. *All* children need to be made aware of the widest possible range of art forms and practices from different cultural contexts. It is still not unheard of (though things are changing – see Gaine 2005) for schools to justify a monocultural, ethnocentric approach to education on the grounds that there are no children from black and Asian communities in their school. This is to miss the point in terms of equal opportunities. It is the children from the majority ethnic group who arguably have a greater need to be introduced to the art forms and the work of practitioners beyond their own cultural framework and for the value of these to be demonstrated by their teachers, to ensure that they are not denied the opportunity to learn about the diversity of cultural traditions in the UK and throughout the world. It is part of teachers' wider responsibility to ensure that children do not acquire the kinds of prejudice that give rise to social injustice. There are plenty of relevant sources that teachers can find and use (see, for example, Jain 1998, Fisher 1984, Penney 1994). Again, many art forms – such as weaving and woodcarving – have been devalued through being designated as craft, or even as 'primitive' art. Some significant forms of art and design, such as architecture, jewellery and mask making are sometimes not even recognized as art practices and some are seen as peripheral art forms because they are non-permanent – such as Mendhi painting and Rangoli pattern making. It is all too easy for teachers to ignore the art and design practices beyond those with which they are familiar, since the art work that dominates in the UK still tends to be of European or American origin, but there are many museums and galleries that celebrate work from a range of cultural contexts and teachers should make sure they use these as a resource wherever possible. Cultural diversity is also increasingly represented in high-profile exhibitions in museums and galleries through the work of artists from otherwise marginalized groups. Examples are the Frida Kahlo exhibition which took place at the Tate Modern in London in 2005 and the Royal Academy exhibition, in the same year, entitled 'Turks: A journey of a thousand years'. Children could be taken to suitable exhibitions of this kind to broaden their experience. It must be borne in mind, however, that this might perpetuate the perception of London museums and galleries as the 'centre' and the more localized experience as 'other', so teachers should also value the galleries and museums in their own region for culturally enriching art and design.

Even within the majority ethnic traditions, some forms of art and design, perhaps identified with 'higher' forms of culture, such as painting and sculpture, are valued over others, such as film and photography, graphic design, furniture design, fashion design, book illustration, product design such as cars and household goods, garden design, packaging and interior decoration (the list can go on). This hierarchy again reflects prejudice and cultural preferences. To raise children's awareness of the diversity of existing art forms, the range of areas to which they are introduced should be consciously extended by teachers to include the less obvious. Working with a wider range of references helps children not only to see the all-pervasiveness of visual culture, but helps to challenge the perception that art and design is an elitist subject. The issue of elitism is pervasive. On the one hand, many museums and galleries are extending the cultural range of work that is made available, creating more opportunities to provide children with first hand experience that broadens their conceptions of art and its cultural origins. On the other hand, however, museums and galleries can, by their very existence, reify certain forms of art, by taking them out of context and implicitly suggesting that art is an interest for a privileged minority, so there is a need to think carefully about the way art and design is presented to children.

Box 8.3 A first step in considering the kind of art and design to introduce

- Is the selection limited to elitist European traditions?
- Can opportunities be made for experiencing art in other contexts (as well as galleries and museums) – in shops and streets, for example?

Through developing a programme of study that focuses on cultural breadth and a range of traditions, not only can children experience a richer variety of approaches, but they can also be helped to understand the ways art forms and practices are interconnected with cultural contexts. It has already been made clear that the pervasive question 'What is art?' has no single answer. Coming to understand the ways in which the values, practices and conventions of a culture have helped to shape the art practices and conceptions of art within it helps children to make sense of art and artworks and to see that art can carry different meanings in different contexts. Taking Aboriginal art in Australia for instance: while Westerners, familiar with the abstraction of Western modernism, might bring to it their appreciation of its apparently abstract form, its cultural significance is very different to the artists who made it. It carries meanings that are related to specific Aboriginal stories and traditions (Isaacs 1984). Teachers have a responsibility not to impose a single, or ethnocentric, way of interpreting artwork, but to help children to gain insight into the different ways that meaning is constructed in different cultural contexts. They need to ensure that children understand something about the people who produced the work, the time and place in which it was made and why it was made. It is important for children to see that the understanding they have of others' work is inevitably partial, as they are seeing it from their own cultural perspective, but that, in this way, they can become aware that there are different conceptions of art. This approach can contribute to their learning about cultural diversity and help them develop a wider perspective as global citizens.

Special educational needs

In mainstream schools there are children in each class of varying abilities. Providing equal opportunities for all the children in a class requires the teacher to have a detailed knowledge of individual children and their needs and to ensure that their teaching responds to each child so they can reach their full potential. As a general principle, all children should be educated according to their individual needs, but there are some who have 'special educational needs' which must be met.

There are some common misconceptions that need to be avoided when thinking about children with special needs in art and design education. One is that children who have learning difficulties, say, in one area, will also have difficulties in art and design. The problem is that the child's difficulties in a particular area (often language and literacy) can be used to ascribe a general label, which in turn influences the way the child's achievements are viewed in other areas. A second misconception is that children with physical disabilities necessarily have special needs. When the child is provided with standard aids, such as a wheelchair, a hearing aid or glasses, there may be no need for any additional resources or provision. Again, the disability label can create barriers that don't exist and, if teachers are not careful, can unnecessarily limit the child's participation in activities.

It is crucial not to create a deficit view of the child as a person as a result of specific characteristics.

Student teachers and teachers are expected to be familiar with the General Teaching Requirements of the National Curriculum, which put forward three principles for inclusion:

- Set suitable learning challenges for all pupils;
- Respond to pupils' diverse needs;
- Overcome potential barriers to learning and assessment for individuals and groups of pupils. (See DfEE/QCA 1999.)

Setting suitable learning challenges for all pupils implies that both the content of the curriculum and teaching approaches will need to be adapted to the needs of individuals. Again the open-endedness of art and design, in accommodating individual responses, suggests that adapting the curriculum for individual needs is already part of teaching in this area. Teachers should, in any case, be sensitive to children's different strengths – they may have particular ability in one area of art and design, but not in others. In responding to diverse strengths and needs, teachers must find ways of differentiating their teaching so that children can continue to build on their achievements to experience success and develop confidence, but also so that they can learn more about those aspects that they find more difficult.

Differentiation

Differentiation where children work on a common task, but where the outcome in part will be dependent on the child's own ability level, is called 'differentiation by outcome'. This method could be seen as an easy option that does not require the teacher to reflect upon this aspect of planning: it treats all the children as if they were the same and lets them find their own level. However, there are positive reasons for adopting this approach. It can often be an ideal form of differentiation for creative subjects, including art and design, where multiple and diverse outcomes are expected and valued from a common creative stimulus or starting point. If activities are well chosen and suitably open-ended it means that children have the opportunity to reach their potential. They are not prevented from achieving what they are capable of, as they might be if they were given prescribed tasks that were insufficiently challenging. Rather than being an approach for unreflective teachers, on the contrary, it requires in-depth knowledge of individual children and their abilities as well as understanding and knowledge of the subject. It demands activities that are planned to be genuinely open-ended and challenging, to enable each child to make real progress.

To help children to do this, teacher interventions must be at just the right level, responsive to the child's developing ideas, skills and knowledge. This demands great skill on the part of the teacher, who must find ways of helping the child to develop creative ideas and resolve problems without imposing their own solutions. All this must be carefully tailored to what the child is trying to achieve and aimed to take their thinking and abilities further. This is also a form of differentiation: differentiation *by support*. At times it will be appropriate to differentiate *by task*, where some children need a different kind of task to ensure that they make progress in their learning.

Teachers need to be aware not only of the special needs of children who, for example, have learning difficulties of different kinds, but also those who are particularly able. Such children – sometimes called 'gifted' and 'talented' – should be challenged in terms of both breadth and depth. It is not always apparent when children are very able but are underachieving – they may, for instance, appear to be inattentive, but are in reality bored through lack of challenging teaching.

Curriculum content and teaching approaches can be designed to extend, enrich or accelerate learning experiences for particularly able children. In setting suitable learning challenges, teachers can select content from the National Curriculum programmes of study from earlier or later Key Stages if necessary. A flexible approach can be adopted to the National Curriculum, for instance where there is insufficient time for particular children with special needs to cover the whole of a programme of study.

Strategies for inclusion

It is a requirement of the National Curriculum that teachers should plan for all to take part. They need to review their curriculum plans to identify any areas that may present particular difficulties to children with special needs and adapt their plans as necessary. The National Curriculum (DfEE/QCA 1999) states that they should respond to children's diverse needs by making the following provision for children:

- Creating effective learning environments
- Securing their motivation and concentration
- Providing equality of opportunity through teaching approaches
- Using appropriate assessment approaches
- Setting targets for learning.

DfEE/QCA (1999)

In practice, this means that, as in the case of ethnic diversity and gender, teachers should always challenge stereotypical views. It has already been suggested that positive images can be used to create open attitudes to diversity in society and also to diversity amongst artists, creating positive role models for all pupils. This extends to those who have special needs. An example is provided by Mark Quinn's sculpture of Alison Lapper which is, at the time of writing, mounted on the fourth plinth in Trafalgar Square. It is a powerful representation of a person with physical disabilities who is herself an artist. Meeting and working with local, practising artists who have special needs can also provide positive experiences. Such strategies will help children to see that all in our society make a valid contribution. Within the classroom, those with special needs should feel the same way. There are many practical ways in which the teacher can make sure that all children feel valued. Given the nature of art and design, the work of children who may have learning difficulties, emotional and behavioural difficulties or physical disabilities can be reviewed and celebrated on an equal basis with that of any other child – for instance, when discussing each other's ideas or in a class display. A child may have a special skill, which comes from having greater experience in a particular area, that they can share with other children. For example, a child with visual impairment may be gaining more experience and skill with three-dimensional work than in drawing and painting and may have a higher level of achievement in this area than some of their friends.

There are teaching and learning strategies which should be adopted to ensure that all children are motivated and participating. For those who have sensory impairment of any kind, the teacher should ensure that all available senses can be used. Experiences that stimulate ideas, and the media through which to develop and communicate them, should be chosen to suit the child. For instance, where there is a focus on observation, the child with visual impairment may need to respond to tactile experiences or sound and may need to work with malleable media; the child with hearing impairment may need more than verbal instructions for a task and may respond well to a focus on observation. Large-scale work may suit those with limited fine motor skills, and small-scale work may suit those with limited mobility. A strength of art and design is that it draws on a variety of sensory experience – touch, as well as sight – and with newer forms, such as installation, sound and movement, and possibly smell and taste. Pace of work needs to be taken into account, too. Some children may need to work at a slower pace. Chapter 4 presents approaches to organization that can accommodate the different rates at which children might work.

There may be children in a class who need specialist equipment or approaches, or adapted activities. Sometimes this may not be immediately obvious. For instance, a child may suffer from allergies to materials used in art and design work, and may need to be provided with protective gloves. Others may not be able to use particular tools owing to physical difficulties. If adapted equipment can be supplied to enable the child to participate, this should be the first course of action, rather than excluding the child from the activity. Some children may well be able to handle paint, but need to have larger brushes that can be easily grasped; visually impaired children may be able to engage in close observation if they are provided with magnifying glasses. Sometimes it won't be possible to make all activities accessible to all children, in which case a suitable, and if possible, equivalent alternative activity should be provided. When taking children out of the classroom for experiences related to art and design, thought needs to be given to what kind of experience will be available for all the children in the class. Teachers must ensure that those with special needs can benefit along with their peers. For example, if an autistic child requires one-to-one supervision, then this needs to be taken into account and, for the visually impaired child, a gallery visit should include worthwhile learning opportunities, such as tactile experiences.

Summary

Art and design has potential to help all children to think about meaning making in its richness and diversity. It's important for teachers to be aware of possible bias and stereotyping in relation to individual children and in terms of the subject matter that is taught. Teachers need to challenge constantly their own ways of thinking and their own actions to avoid perpetuating inequalities or imposing limits on children's learning.

For further reading, a useful discussion of multicultural education in art and design can be found in Mason (1995).

Bibliography

Cox, S. (2005), 'Intention and meaning in young children's drawing', in *International Journal of Art and Design Education* 24 (2): 115–25.

DfEE/QCA (1999), *The National Curriculum – Handbook for Primary Teachers in England – Key Stages 1 and 2*. London: DfEE/QCA.

Fisher, A. (1984), *Africa Adorned*. London: Collins.

Gaine, C. (2005), *We're All White, Thanks – The Persisting Myth About White Schools*. Stoke on Trent: Trentham Books.

Herne, S. (ed.) (1995), *Art in the Primary School*. London: Borough of Tower Hamlets.

Isaacs, J. (1984), *Australia's Living Heritage – Arts of the Dreaming*. Sydney: Landsdowne.

Jain, J. (ed.) (1998), *Other Masters: Five Contemporary Folk and Tribal Artists of India*. New Delhi: Crafts Museum and The Handicrafts and Handloom Exports Corporation of India Ltd.

Kress, G. (1997), *Before Writing: Re-thinking the Paths to Literacy*. London: Routledge.

Mason, R. (1995), *Art Education and Multiculturalism (2nd edition)*. Corsham: National Society for Education in Art and Design.

Parker, R. and Pollock, G. (1981), *Old Mistresses: Women, Art and Ideology*. London: Pandora.

Penney, D. (1994), *Native American Art*. Cologne: Konemann.

QCA/DfEE (2000), *Curriculum Guidance for the Foundation Stage*. London: QCA/DfEE.

Sterling, S. F. (1995), *Women Artists – The National Museum of Women in the Arts*. New York: Abbeville.

Appendix: Resources

Drawing/mark making

Conventional drawing materials

Aquarelle (water-based) pencils

Chalk pastels

Charcoal – thick sticks, thin sticks

Chunky graphite sticks

Conté crayons

Felt tip pens – from fine-line to bold markers

Inks – a range of colours, etc.

Ink pens

Oil pastels

Pencils (2H, HB to 6B)

Pencil crayons

Wax crayons

Non-conventional drawing materials

Some ideas: a collection of natural and non-natural artefacts with interesting textures, shapes, colours, patterns – bark, wood grain, shells, rocks, seeds, fabric, machinery, (see suggested list in Drawing section of 'Processes' chapter)

Artstraws/matchsticks/cotton buds

Feathers

Forks

Nail brushes

Pebbles/stones

Sticks

The following can help with observation:

Magnifying lenses

Mirrors

Viewfinders

Painting

Paints: (colours: brilliant blue , turquoise, crimson,vermilion, brilliant yellow, lemon yellow, black, white)

Acrylic (Chromacryl) liquid paint

Powder colours

Ready mixed paints

Tempera blocks

Watercolour blocks/tins

Palettes, etc.

8-well palettes for tempera blocks

Disposable palette sheets

Palettes – some divided in to circular sections for powder paints, others flat and rectangular

Small pots for mixing and keeping colours

Paper

Brown packing paper

Card

Cartridge paper – A2 A3 A4.

Sugar paper/Brushwork paper – grey, white, black, and a range of sizes and colours, including large rolls

Tissue paper (range of colours)

Brushes: large, small, thick, thin, hog hair/sable (or equivalent, such as nylon)

Miscellaneous

Aprons

Plastic water pots (stable)

Tools for 'non-conventional' painting – marbles, sticks, glue-spreaders, card, sticks, etc.

Washing up liquid – mix with powder paints

Printmaking

Biros or sharp, hard pencils (2H) for press prints

Block printing inks (water-based)

Card

Craft knives for collographs

Cutting mats

Double-sided sellotape

Fabric for printing on – e.g. cotton lawn

Finger paints for mono prints

Flat rectangular palettes (or off-cuts of plastic sheeting or Perspex or floor tiles) for rolling out inks

Lino

Lino cutting tools (and bench hooks)

Plastic or metal palette knives for mixing inks

Polystyrene tiles for press prints (the ones made for the purpose – ordinary polystyrene tiles from DIY shops do not have a smooth enough surface)

Potatoes

Range of papers, including newsprint and tissue

Rollers

Screens for silk screen-printing or wooden frames and organza to stretch own screens

Sheets of Perspex for monoprints

Silk screen-printing ink (water based)

Squeegees for silk screen-printing

Sticky backed brown paper tape, for sealing edges of screens

String

Tissues

Unit-printing: cotton reels, Lego bricks, toy cars, corks, 'junk' items, string wrapped around wood blocks, etc.

Vegetables

Water colour paints or dyes for painting over rubbings (wax resist)

Wax crayons for rubbings

Sculpture

A bench for using resistant materials with a vice and bench-hooks

Card

Cardboard boxes and rolls

Chicken wire

Coldwater paste (Wallpaper paste without the fungicide)

Corrugated card

Foam board

Glue gun

Masking tape

Mod-Roc

Newspaper

Pipe cleaners

Plaster of Paris

Plastic bottles

Plastic buckets for papier mâché

Plasticine

PVA glue

Recycled materials; junk, etc.

Sand

Soap, plaster, leather hard clay for carving

Tin foil

Tools – saws, hammers, pliers, screwdrivers, hand drills, nails, screws, etc.

Wire and wire cutters

Wood

Wood blocks

Clay/modelling materials

23-litre plastic bin for recycled clay

A kiln for firing

Batt wash – shelves need to be painted with batt wash periodically to help prevent glaze from sticking to shelves.

Boards

'Cheese wire' cutters for cutting clay

Clay that doesn't require firing

Clay, e.g. earthenware (kept in airtight bags) 'white' (grey before firing) or 'red' (terracotta colour) – white allows for the use of under-glaze paints

Collection of 'random bits' for impressing marks into clay, e.g. small shells, keys, dried pasta shapes, screws, etc.

Glaze – e.g. transparent glaze and coloured glaze

Kiln 'furniture': shelving or 'batts'; supports for shelves (these come in different sizes and fit together so they can be built up to provide the height of shelf required); ceramic 'stilts' (of different sizes) on which to stand glazed work in the kiln – to prevent them from sticking to the shelf during firing

Mop brushes for applying glaze

Plastic buckets for mixing glaze, re-constituting dried clay, mixing batt-wash, etc.

Plasticine

Playdough – commercially produced or homemade

Potters' sieves for mixing glaze

Rolling pins and 'tram lines'

Soft brushes for applying under-glaze paints and glazes

Specialist tools for scooping out clay (hollowing out clay items)

Sponges

Supplies of plastic bags and flexible wire fasteners (to keep closed and airtight) for storing work in progress

Tools: lollipop sticks, cocktail sticks, scoops, blunt knives, plastic or wooden specialist tools

Under-glaze paints

Collage

Foil, threads, fibres, fabrics, plastic, wood, metal, stone, shells, pulses, feathers, grasses

Glue spreaders, glue sticks

Hand-painted papers

Magazines

Newspapers

PVA glue, plastic glue pots or yoghurt pot containers

Range of coloured paper and card – new and recycled scraps

Sheets of acetate for tissue collage work (or dustbin liners for large scale work)

Tissue paper – range of colours

Textiles

Batik tools (*tjanting* tools)

Cotton string (which the children can dip-dye themselves)

Drawing pins to fasten fabric to stretchers

Dressmakers' pins

Fabric dyes – range of colours (Reeves Craft Dyes for fabric painting; Dylon cold water dyes for dip dying, tie-dye, batik; specialist ready-mixed dyes for batik can provide stronger colours)

Fine cotton lawn for batik (cotton fabric is also best for any work where cold water dyes are used.)

Iron for removing wax from batik.

Needles (range of sizes for different thicknesses of thread and wool, including tapestry needles), thimbles, knitting needles

Old picture frames, PE hoops, redundant bicycle wheels, forked branches, etc. for use as looms for weaving; card looms

Plain newsprint paper for the process of removing wax

Raffia

Range of fabrics for printing, batik, collage and embroidery, including felt. Fabric interfacing (non woven) is good for some transfer fabric crayons.

Scissors that are reserved for fabric use only; some larger shears for cutting large pieces of fabric; possibly pinking shears as well

Sewing machine in KS2 will open up a wider range of possibilities including machine embroidery.

Stretchers for fabric for batik work

Threads, collection of coloured wools for weaving and embroidery

Various fabric paints and crayons from suppliers (applied in different ways according to instructions)

Wadding

Wax (paraffin wax or specialist batik wax)

Wax kettles or stoves

Wax pellets, blocks or candles for simplified batik work

Wooden boards (prevent wax dripping on tables)

ICT

Software (suggested)

Adobe Photoshop

Dazzle Plus

I can animate

Paint Shop Pro

Revelation Natural Art

Hardware

'Digital Blue' or equivalent camera for animation

Digital camera (with manual function)

Digital Video Camera

Interactive whiteboard, projector

Memory Stick

Scanner/printer (A3 if budget will allow)/copier

Tripod

Video camera

Visual resources

Books on a range of artists and designers

DVDs, videos

Examples of original textile work; sculpture; paintings; drawings, cultural artefacts, etc. (some museums and galleries have a lending scheme; sometimes the local authority or teachers' centre have such items for loan)

Packs of reproduced art works and other images, etc. (there is a wide range available)

Other resources

Drying rack

Frames for paper making

Marbling inks

Masking tape

Metal rulers

Paper clips

Paper fasteners

Rotary trimmer

Sellotape

Staple gun

Useful organizations, schemes, projects

The Artist Teacher Scheme

The Artist Teacher Scheme is an expanding programme of continuing professional development courses devised by partnerships between galleries or museums and university schools of fine art and design to enable teachers to regain or develop their personal practice as artists.

http://www.nsead.org/cpd/

Artscape – the National Directory for the Arts

The artscape directory features organizations and individual artists who undertake educational work. All artforms and regions are covered and many more artists and organizations are currently being added. They ensure that all individuals who are available for work in schools have Enhanced Disclosure checks. You will also find two references from previous employers published as part of each directory entry.

http://www.artscape.org.uk/

Artsmark – recognition and reward for schools dedicated to the arts

An Artsmark is awarded to schools who show a commitment to the full range of arts – music, dance, drama and art & design. It is a national award scheme and is managed by Arts Council England.The Artsmark is available to all schools in England. It is awarded after an application, assessment and validation process.

http://www.artscouncil.org.uk/artsmark/

Drumcroon Gallery – Universal Themes Links pages

The Universal Themes were formulated by Rod Taylor as a means by which the art of the world across time, place and culture can be grouped together, with two or more themes being present in many.

http://www.drumcroon.org.uk/Resource/themes/universalthemes.html

London Schools Arts Service

LONSAS is the leading online arts and education resource for London schools and artists. They matchmake schools with artists and arts organizations, promoting creative opportunities and academic achievement throughout the curriculum.

http://www.lonsas.org.uk/

National Curriculum in Action – Art & Design

This website uses pupils' work and case study materials to show what the National Curriculum in art and design looks like in practice. The examples given show: the standard of pupils' work at different ages and Key Stages; how the programmes of study translate into real activities; and the effective use of ICT across the curriculum.

http://www.ncaction.org.uk/subjects/art/

National Curriculum Online – Art & Design

http://www.nc.uk.net/nc/contents/AD-home.htm

National Society for Education in Art and Design

The NSEAD is the leading national authority concerned with art, craft and design across all phases of education in the United Kingdom. They offer, for a single subscription, the extensive benefits of membership of a professional association, a learned society and a trade union. START (published by the NSEAD) is an exciting and stimulating magazine for teachers of pre-school and primary art, craft and design first published in 2003. Published twice a term, START is full of ideas and resources intended to support classroom practice. The International Journal of Art & Design Education (previously the 'Journal of Art & Design Education') provides an international forum for the dissemination of ideas, practical developments, and research findings in art and design education. The Journal (published under the auspices of the NSEAD) is a primary source for independently refereed articles about art and design education at all levels.

http://www.nsead.org

Standards for QTS and requirements for ITT

The standards and requirements in this document replace DfEE Circular 4/98 and have the same legal standing. They set out: the Secretary of State's standards, which must be met by trainee teachers before they can be awarded qualified teacher status; the requirements for training providers and those who make recommendations for the award of qualified teacher status. Only those trainee teachers who have met all of the standards will be awarded qualified teacher status (QTS). (Note: at the time or writing these standards and requirements were under review. The draft version of the revised standards is referred to in this book, also available on this website.)

http://www.tda.gov.uk/partners/ittstandards.aspx

Teaching Ideas – Art

A website set up by a primary teacher in the UK with contributions from many practising teachers.

http://www.teachingideas.co.uk/art/contents.htm

Index